SISTER WISDOM

---

7 PATHWAYS TO A SATISFYING LIFE FOR SOULFUL BLACK WOMEN

Patricia Reid-Merritt

John Wiley & Sons, Inc.

To

Belinda Faye Merritt Wetzel

*Whose premature and untimely passing snatched away
any opportunity that we might have had
to share fond memories of the prime*

Published by John Wiley & Sons, Inc., New York
Published simultaneously in Canada

ISBN 0471-41724-6

Printed in the United States of America

10 9 8 7 6 5 4 3 2 1

Contents

Preface

The strong black woman is dead!
On August 15, 1999, at 11:55 p.m., while struggling
with the reality of being a human being instead of a
myth, the strong black woman passed away, without the
slightest bit of hoopla.
Medical sources say that she died of natural causes, but
those who know and used her know what she died from.

I t was merely the beginning of a long, passionate poem that
reflected a revolution in the attitudes of millions of African
American women. The unknown poet tapped a deep vein of
frustration and sorrow. Here was an outpouring of pent-up,
unexpressed, raw emotion instantly recognizable to every self-
respecting black woman in America over the age of thirty.

She died from loving men who didn't love themselves and
could only offer her a crippled reflection.
She died from raising children alone and for not doing a
complete job.
She died from the lies her grandmother told her mother
and her mother told her about life, men and racism.
She died from being a mother at 15 and a grandmother
at 30 and an ancestor at 45.
She died from being dragged down and sat upon by UN-
evolved women posing as sisters.

She died from pretending the life she was living was a
Kodak moment instead of a 20th century, post-slavery
nightmare!!!

Yet the anonymous poet closed on a defiant note. And it
was her parting line that struck the resounding chord:

The strong, silent, s———t-taking Black woman is dead!
Or is she still alive and kicking? I know I'm still here.

In the cool, crisp days that marked the beginning of fall
and, ironically, in the final months of the old millennium, the
poem hit the Internet. E-mail was forwarded from daughters
to mothers and among friends in sister circles throughout the
nation.

In chat rooms and discussion groups, there grew the
mounting expression of an urgent desire and willingness to
unmask the mythical fast-talking, finger-shaking, hip-swinging,
mule-of-the-earth, superstrong black woman. Black women
everywhere welcomed the strong black woman's obituary with
lightning speed. Silent in her suffering, the mythical sister
was dead. Alive and kicking, soulful sisters cried, "Amen." The
word went out that it was no longer necessary or possible to
preserve an image of superior strength and supreme sacrifice.
We refused to define ourselves by our pain anymore.

My observation of this extraordinary national dialogue
gave focus and direction to this book. It is a book for and about
millions of increasingly savvy and sophisticated African American women who are in the process of breaking free from a

haunted memory. Virtually unheralded, these sisters have created a new era in black female identity.

Like most women in this vanguard, I am a member of what I call "Generation Midlife," a 1950s baby boomer who's done some living. While a great deal of literature has proliferated about the needs and demands of the nation's boomers, few, if any, studies have been made about us—approximately five million black women who are somewhere between our thirties and fifties.

Based on the evidence of our reaction to the poem on the Internet, the role of the mythical strong black woman has lost its hold on us. More life-sustaining roles have taken its place. We no longer put up with anxiety, stress, and confusion the way we used to. We crave and are driving toward something better in life. Skeptics might say that this phenomenon is natural and unremarkable. But, overwhelmingly, black women themselves describe it as a source of new knowledge, unexpected freedom, and hope.

How is it that black women over thirty manage to save themselves from despair? When did we stop believing our own myth? What images inspire us now? How do we restructure our relationships and make room for our genuine presence? How much happier are we willing to try to be? Based on my research into the life experiences of my pioneering, over-thirty-something generation, *Sister Wisdom* offers answers and insights for the benefit of sisters of all ages.

By candidly sharing typical life stories, I hope to quicken the arrival of the day when all sisters see beyond their present dilemmas and issues and become aware that every woman has a right to future happiness and can choose her pathway to it.

In fact, the evidence you will find in the pages of *Sister Wisdom* suggests that in order to have a happy, satisfying life, you *must* choose a pathway. While no pathway is perfect or permanent, seven have emerged in my research as being intuitive and healing for most black women. At different stages of our lives, one or more of these pathways will beckon. I will discuss this phenomenon in depth throughout this book.

I want you to acknowledge your own power to know what's right for you now and to embrace any pathway of your choice. I also want to encourage you to change pathways in times of self-doubt. I want to inspire you to lay down your burden and give up business as usual, if that's what it takes to be as satisfied as you want to be. These are not my mother's stories but stories told by a generation of women with higher expectations for a deeply satisfying life. I think these stories prove what the wisest of our foremothers have always known: that women who make bold choices quickly recover their dignity, self-respect, and an unbridled love for the inherent value and worth of their sisterhood.

As you come through whatever emotional territory you find yourself in today, use this book to renew your spirit. Gain further insight into life-poisoning choices and stifling relationships. Create a sharper vision of your future possibilities. Prepare for tomorrow's inevitable challenges. See how necessary it is for you to make bold moves to lay claim to a satisfying life of your own.

Acknowledgments

I was in the midst of writing my grandmother's memoir when I received the call from literary agent Barbara Lowenstein testing my interest in this project.

"Where are the books for black women looking for a good life beyond their twenties?" she asked. "Would you be interested in working on a project that focuses on the experiences of these women?"

I jumped at the chance. I thank Barbara and her business partner, Madeleine Morel, for stimulating my interest.

Still, it's a long road to travel from idea to completion of a project. This book would not have been possible without the support, encouragement, and challenges that I received from my editor, Carole Hall, at John Wiley & Sons. Carole was able to grasp my vision from the very beginning and was willing to work with me as I made my way through. I am deeply appreciative of her support.

I extend my deepest thanks and appreciation to all the sisters who allowed me in their personal, private spaces and shared their stories with me. It was a fascinating journey that revealed the depth and richness of our collective experiences. This book would not have existed without their honest contributions and insights on issues that confront contemporary black women.

I am also deeply indebted to all the sisters who responded via e-mail. What a blast! I learned firsthand the awesome power of the Internet and the information superhighway. It allowed me to reach sisters beyond my initially anticipated capacity.

While I had an abundance of true-life material, I still needed help pulling together all of the research materials necessary to frame the discussion on sisters' lives. I am especially thankful for the support I received from my research assistants, Tia Josephs and Samaiyah Clayton. These two senior students at Richard Stockton College of New Jersey demonstrated the value of a strong undergraduate education and proved to me that research opportunities should not be limited to students on the graduate level.

Several women read the manuscript in various stages of the project and offered constructive feedback. I am particularly grateful to Michele Lyons Nicholson, Dr. Adele Newsome-Horst, Josleen Wilson, Dr. Linda Nelson, Vanessa Lloyd-Sbamati, and many others for taking time out of their busy schedules to comment on the structure and style of the book.

There were so many sister friends who supported my efforts. It's too difficult to name them all. A special thanks to Dr. Charlotte Thomas-Hawkins, Sharon Ingram-Nix, Earnestine Simpson-Steverson, Professor Adele Beverly, Karen Thompson, and Carolyn Lurry-Mapp, Esq., who provided a sounding board throughout the process; to Dr. Julianne Malveaux, who used her strong national network of sister friends to help get the word out on the need for sisters to respond to my request for input; to Sisterspace and Books for their support and encouragement; and to Anita Craig and

ACKNOWLEDGMENTS

Maxine Brown, who reminded me that true friendships always endure the test of time.

The past year has been stressful in many ways. Family members and close friends nurtured me through a difficult grieving process. I love you much.

I am blessed to have a daughter, Christina Bookhart, whose language and editing skills are far superior to my own. I am indebted to her for the many hours that she spent working with me. And I hope her work on this project inspires her to write her own book.

Finally, my heartfelt thanks to my son, Brahim Khari Bookhart, and stepsons Gregory Merritt and Jeffrey Merritt. And to my husband, Bill—you were always there for me. Your love is the most meaningful aspect of my life.

PART ONE

Our Challenges

1

The Satisfying Life

Imagine finally being free to be all that you want to be. Imagine waking up grateful for a renewed beginning. Your inner voice sings to you: This is the good life. You look forward to engaging it to its fullest. You don't need to cry about finding your space; you have it. You have created your own world by making bold and sometimes unconventional choices to guarantee your well-being. This book is about how forty-two African American women achieved this kind of satisfaction, and you can too.

Two years ago, I began looking for self-assured, self-nurturing black women who were living the good life on their own terms. I was on a mission to find sisters who would be gracious enough to share the secret of their peace and freedom with me, and no sister was safe from my quest. I approached anyone and everyone who looked like "they had done some living" and encouraged them to tell me their life stories. I went wherever black women gathered to relax, talk to each other, congratulate each other, and celebrate their survival: birthday parties, rites-of-passage programs, sister circle parties, book signings, professional meetings, and conferences.

In August 2000, I found the largest gathering of black women in the city of Atlanta. T. D. Jakes's spiritual revival, *Woman, Thou Art Loosed*, drew more than eighty thousand attendees. Sisters imbued with the spirit of the Lord were ubiquitous. They filled every street in downtown Atlanta, and the energy in the convention center was overwhelming. These sisters were seeking inspiration, spiritual healing, fellowship, and, according to one sister from Indianapolis, Indiana, "a deeper understanding of the hurt and pain I've experienced in life." Teens through senior citizens had traveled by train, air, car, bus, and subway. Church vans and buses marked First Baptist, Second Baptist, and Christ Baptist waited in the lots of hotels and motels in and around the greater metropolitan area. All over town, I left flyers announcing my intentions and begging sisters to "talk to me." Back at home in New Jersey, I sent e-mail messages and extended personal invitations to friends, foes, and colleagues asking for their support.

By fall, 110 women responded to my appeal. Their messages arrived via e-mail, telephone, and the U.S. Postal Service. These sisters were self-selected and yet diverse: professionals and nonprofessionals, career women and housewives, single women and married women, and mothers and childless women. They represented every region in the country. Some provided short anecdotes about life's joys and pleasures; others offered lengthy narratives of their efforts to reach and traverse the midlife divide successfully.

I responded to every contact. Eventually, I conducted face-to-face and/or telephone interviews with forty-two women. These in-depth interviews afforded us the opportunity for further exploration and discovery. I sought clarification of each sister's original responses and a deeper understanding of her views not only on what constituted a good life for her but how she achieved it.

The interviews lasted anywhere from one to three hours. Everyone expressed great concern about privacy and confidentiality. "I'm telling you stuff that I've only told to my therapist," one sister told me. "I hope you know what to do with it." I guaranteed each person her anonymity in this book.

THE POWER OF CHOOSING YOUR ROLE

After so many conversations, I found the secret that I'd been looking for. Over and over, I heard satisfied women express making choices to organize their lives around one key role. As I looked at some of the roles the women played at home or in their careers, for example, I thought, that particular role would never work for me, but I could understand the happiness that it brought women for whom it was exactly right.

A person's social role is a pathway, for it is through it that one discovers and channels a personal vision of the good life. The truth is that there are many different pathways to a satisfying life. No pathway is superior to the others. All that matters is whether that pathway is in sync with our needs and personalities. Most people will try more than one pathway before finding one where everything clicks. Pursuing the right pathway gives us the sense of purpose and self-worth that is the essence of satisfaction.

This understanding led me to look more closely at the stories I had gathered, and when I did so, I could see that seven roles—or pathways—were most frequently reported by the satisfied sisters I had interviewed.

THE PATHWAY OF THE DOMESTIC WARRIOR

Domestic warriors were sisters whose primary energies were focused on their homes and families. It is a very traditional role, yet for black women it lacks social recognition and cultural supports. It is not, for the most part, a role that has been inherited from our mothers.

Domestic warriors are descendants from a long line of working black women whose menial paychecks from low-status jobs were needed to help the family survive. However, today's sister warriors have chosen to devote their full-time efforts to the nurturing and protection of their children and family. They are financially supported in this choice by working husbands.

On the whole, these sisters are acutely aware of the challenges of black family life in America and understand the social ramifications of race and racism. They are careful to examine daily incidents for telltale signs of bias and discrimination, willing to fight for the needs of their families, and committed to producing a healthy generation of responsible young people.

THE PATHWAY OF THE SINGLE-PARENT PROFESSIONAL

Single-parent professionals were sisters who by choice or life circumstances assumed primary responsibility for raising and providing for their offspring. Like domestic warriors, they were extremely devoted to their children. Their distinction from their sisters who were devoted to home and family rests in the fact that single parenthood made them financially responsible and uniquely accountable.

Many sisters have concluded that the lack of available male partners to assume the role of father and husband is a function of race, racism, and the socialization process. However, the single-parent professional can and will raise her child alone and is confident of her ability to do so. Through a series of wise educational and career choices, she has secured a satisfying professional position that affords her the advantages or serious hope of a middle-class lifestyle.

Poverty as a major social obstacle has been eliminated in this sister's household through her own efforts and the support of those around her. This major factor differentiates these sisters from the many single black females raising children in poverty without adequate social resources and suffering from onerous economic hardship.

THE PATHWAY OF THE INDEPENDENT FREE FLOATER

Independent free floaters were sisters at the center of their own lives. This pathway emphasizes self and pleasure. Some of these sisters had never been married; others were previously married and are widowed or divorced. Some never had children, whereas others successfully ushered their grown children out of the household.

While it might seem that everyone has the potential for total freedom, these sisters have chosen to exercise it. They pick and choose how they wish to spend their time, resources, and personal energy. Their needs are second to none, and they refuse to apologize for occupying a social space that brings them peace, comfort, joy, and sheer pleasure. Independent free floaters are bodacious. As black women, they recognize the power of their positions: They are emotionally unencumbered sisters with plenty of resources to share.

THE PATHWAY OF THE PASSIONATE SOUL MATE

Passionate soul mates were profoundly in love. Their hearts had been captured by the love of their lives. They were consumed by a personal relationship defined by reciprocity in all areas of life. It is a shared intimacy that most people only dream about. Their partners were male or female and came from various ethnic backgrounds.

Passionate soul mates are fully invested in their relationships and express great joy in existing in a world that grants them the opportunity to be "emotionally naked" in the presence of a loved one. As black women, they categorize their love as a rare exception and treat the bonds of the relationship as sacred.

THE PATHWAY OF THE BLISSFUL WONDER

Blissful wonders were sisters who had achieved a near perfect balance between the needs of their loved ones, their professional careers, and their personal desires. They were the multitasking women who have placed their own needs on the agenda. They frequently used adjectives such as blessed, lucky, and fortunate to describe their current status.

This is the path sisters frequently imagined in their youth, until they found out that they were not the superwomen in other people's imaginations. Blissful wonders' greatest strength lies in their ability to make choices, say no to excessive demands, and shed the unwanted baggage that would burden their lives.

THE PATHWAY OF THE FAITHFUL FOLLOWER

Faithful followers were sisters who derived their strength, direction, salvation, and solution to all problems from God Almighty. He went by many names, including Lord, Jesus,

Jehovah, Allah, Master, and Creator. The power of His spirit was overwhelming for them. Every twist and turn in life could be explained only through acceptance of His infinite wisdom. This was the pathway of living salvation.

Faithful followers are deeply spiritual and believe that God is in control of their choices and potential. As black women, they are embracing a legacy of faith that has anchored the black community throughout the tumultuous reign of terror and oppression that blacks have endured in North America. For the faithful sister, nothing happens without the blessing of God. And she will tell you that He provides all that is needed to enjoy a rich and satisfying life.

THE PATHWAY OF THE SOUL SURVIVOR

Soul survivors were sisters whose daily struggles, social burdens, and personal tragedies provided focus, strength, and new directions. These sisters viewed life as a constant struggle, but believed that they have the ability to overcome life's obstacles.

Soul survivors understand and accept their painful past, readily acknowledge the double-edged effect of being black and female in America, and yet are still comfortably evolving into a new phase of life. They look back and celebrate the fact that they've come this far. They find satisfaction in the fact that their accomplishments in their personal and professional lives are a launching pad for future endeavors.

Their critiques on racism, discrimination, and other forms of social injustice are balanced by honest, forthright revelations about personal choices, personal failures, and secret indiscretions. These sisters do not see themselves as victims or victors but as proud survivors.

The mythical strong black woman lives in their memories because of the hard truth behind her legend. Black women have made many gains, but according to the 2000 census, they continue to hold the lowest-paying domestic and service jobs. Despite important educational gains, sisters continue to earn less than 70 cents for every dollar earned by white males. At a median annual income of less than $23,000, sisters as a whole are among the poorest of all wage-earning Americans. We are least likely to be married and the most likely to have our children living with us in poverty. And many sisters well into their middle years have been forced into the role of primary caretaker and guardian parent as their grandchildren lose their parents to incarceration, drug addiction, and a host of other social problems. In 2001, in the midst of the growing AIDS epidemic, 1 in 180 African American women were HIV positive, compared to 1 in 3,000 white women. Soul survivors find a pathway through such roadblocks because they clear away false assumptions.

FALSE ASSUMPTION NUMBER ONE

"I am too tired, overworked, and overwhelmed to ever be happy."

Almost everybody gripes about something. But many black women may actually have day-to-day burdens that have left them without a glimmer of hope. Either consciously or subconsciously, an accumulation of crises, losses, setbacks, and obstacles could be confining your spirit in a straitjacket of pain and frustration, too.

As a sister, it is important to be open about your problems, and urgent not to let them crush you. You will find assurance here as you read about women who faced many problems and difficult situations yet found their lives transformed as their pathways became clearer.

FALSE ASSUMPTION NUMBER TWO

"The best years of my life are behind (or ahead of) me. I can't be bothered worrying about what's next."

Along with the women whose stories you will hear, I believe that change is the natural order of things. But we help create the future. Whatever your age, you need to check on your memories and dreams periodically in order to see your life anew. When was the last time you asked yourself how you were doing? Are you where you thought you would be at this age? Do you want more joy and happiness? Could your relationships be stronger? These are not questions of biology or chronology but of self-knowledge.

Sister Wisdom is about the knowledge that makes a satisfying life achievable. It is about the necessity to set or reset your direction. Getting where you want to be as soon as you can, and staying there as long as possible, is really what the search for a satisfying life is all about. You have a role to play in creating your own destiny.

FALSE ASSUMPTION NUMBER THREE

"I am already as close as I can get to being satisfied."

Have you ever thought, is this it? Well, maybe it is, and maybe it isn't. The stories in this book show that life is often about taking what you have and making it work for you. But there is always something out there that is much better. Is there something you want to do or somewhere you want to go in life, but you don't know how to get there?

Many of the sisters you will meet on these pages have known that feeling of being stuck at a dead end. But when they found ways to embrace themselves, they discovered that it was possible to let go of unrewarding attachments and move on. Remaining flexible, sisters who ultimately felt satisfaction continued their search for balance, harmony, and inner peace for many years.

Beware of expecting satisfaction to come overnight. It can take many years, even decades.

FALSE ASSUMPTION NUMBER FOUR

"I just want to lead a good life, so I don't need a special pathway."

This assumption is very close to me. I heard this expression a lot when I published my previous book, *Sister Power: How Phenomenal Black Women Are Rising to the Top*. I was thrilled by the enthusiasm with which audiences responded to that book. It's five years later, and I still travel across the country and receive mail from around the world about it. It was about black women's unique style and strategies for leadership as they contend for national and global power.

I frequently heard from sisters for whom power was equally real but private and local. "What about the rest of us who do not aspire to follow in the path of exceptional women?" sisters asked. The answer is here on these pages. Empowering pathways are as comfortable as your own skin. Satisfied sisters are made extraordinary by their ability to thrive.

SISTER WISDOM FOR YOU

As you read, notice how the sisters in the stories are making positive choices to alter the direction of unsatisfying situations. The sisters you are about to meet were bold enough to take action when action was needed.

The collective truth of these bold sisters, reaffirmed by their life experiences, is what I call "sister wisdom." It is the sum of the lessons we acquire on the journey that leads to a life of satisfaction. Notice how sisters gather the wisdom. See how it guides and protects them when they are making life choices.

Sister wisdom grows during six crucial life challenges, starting with childhood. Today's satisfied sisters struggled in childhood to know themselves. How they came to terms with their uniqueness shaped their lives for years. Lest you believe that your emotional foundation was complete when you entered adulthood, it is important to review the challenge of your own identity formation from this vantage point

Next, sister wisdom sees us through the paradox of having built up great hopes for the future. Although today's satisfied sisters were raised on dreams, their youthful dreams rarely matched their adult realities. Embarking on marriage, careers, or higher education, even gifted and remarkably resilient young women were unprepared for the harshness and demands of the world beyond their original family and community relationships. Fortunately, sister wisdom provides regular assurance that no matter what's happening in your world and no matter how vulnerable you feel, you still have choices.

I don't have to tell you that life takes it toll. You have been there along with the women whose stories you are about to hear. Today's satisfied sisters had to loosen the immediate and long-term straitjacketing effect of early decisions regarding marriage and mothering. They had to confront domestic disturbances, private stresses, and seemingly unimaginable life struggles from their twenties through midlife. So as you read on, remember that sister wisdom works. Use it, and your deepest satisfaction will be on its way.

2

The Way We Were:

Accepting Our Unique Selves

O ur faces and those of our sisters are rarely prominent in the books, magazines, and movies that depict American life and history, but we were always there—millions of young black girls trying to find our way.

Each of the women you will meet in this chapter—Ricki, Tea, Terri, Chrystal, Shelli, Judith, and Darla—illuminates something special about a black woman's identity formation process—the foundation for self-discovery, self-acceptance, and self-satisfaction. I hope that reading their stories will evoke memories that reconnect you to your childhood dreams and fantasies.

As children, we gather information from the world and formulate images of who we are and how we fit into the larger scheme of things. We soon discover that the adult world is far from perfect. And like the jagged-edged piece of a jigsaw puzzle that we try to squeeze into every available space, we begin the lifelong process of trying to locate our proper place.

Race and gender have a way of complicating our ability to achieve a healthy, positive sense of self in a timely manner. Negative images of the value and worth of black women cloud our search for an appropriate identity. We are denied social supports that are taken for granted by others. As we mature, unresolved issues and conflicts that we experienced during our childhood may continue to be obstacles to a happy and satisfying life.

BACK IN THE DAY

Every generation has a particular mix of elements that give childhood a special flavor. Sister boomers, for example, were around to help launch the Mickey Mouse Club. Cheryl, Bobby, Annette, Cubby, Doreen, and Darlene were the names we chanted in unison as we glued our faces to 12-inch black-and-white television sets. We watched *Howdy Doody with Buffalo Bob; Kukla, Fran and Ollie; Captain Kangaroo;* and *Mr. Chips.* Television without the benefit of remote control was an integral part of our lives.

We collected the first Barbies and hugged three-foot Patty Play Pal dolls with blonde hair and blue eyes. We loved, cherished, and cared for these dolls. We practiced being good mommies and good homemakers. We baked real cakes in Easy Bake Ovens and cleaned the floor with Little People Sweepers.

But all the dolls were white, all the television people were white, and we were black. All black. A dizzying array of mixed chocolate little girls in search of our own identity.

Saturday morning cartoon shows, where animal figures ruled, offered us some relief. Mickey Mouse was joined by Bugs Bunny, Daffy Duck, Road Runner, Wile E. Coyote, Woody Woodpecker, and Mighty Mouse. In this world of fantasy, race was never an issue. But Little Lulu, Popeye, and Casper the Friendly Ghost placed animation in human context. From the prehistoric Flintstones to the futuristic Jetsons, we were surrounded by subliminal messages that conveyed the insignificance of our existence.

Sister boomers were born to a generation of hardworking, plain-talking people who were aware that the presence of blacks on television was a rarity. We flew down steps, jumped over obstacles, and dropped whatever we were doing when someone in the family shouted, "There's a colored person on TV!" The whole family rushed to the living room to see the black man or woman on the snow-filled, grainy screen.

Our parents loved watching the *Amos and Andy Show* until protests from the black community removed it from the air. And they enjoyed the brief tenure of Nat King Cole, whose show was pulled after one year for lack of commercial sponsorship. But with the exception of *The Little Rascals*, rarely did we see the face of a black child on the wonder box. Most of us were long past our formative years before television offered shows like *Julia* (1968) and *Fat Albert* (1969).

The overwhelming majority of sister boomers were born into two-parent families. Yes, we did know our daddies, although they would die a lot sooner than white daddies. They worked in factories, steel mills, and foundries. They were farmers, maintenance workers, mechanics, and television repairmen. Some were schoolteachers, preachers, and undertakers. Only a select few—less than 2 percent—were in the elite professional job categories of physicians, lawyers, bankers, and college professors.

In the 1950s and 1960s, most black folks lived in residentially segregated areas in the urban North, rural South, burgeoning West, and industrialized Midwest. Black businesses designed to cater to our special interests were available within walking distance. Mom-and-pop grocery stores, neighborhood bars, funeral parlors, barbershops, and beauty shops lined the main business streets up and down our avenue. Often we shared this space with Jewish and Italian families who owned small retail businesses that also catered to blacks. Some of us lived in transitional communities where, for a brief moment, the neighborhoods were racially integrated. This was one of our first encounters with cultural diversity as we witnessed, up close, the difference between white and black lifestyles. There were exceptions in every neighborhood, but there were also rules.

White people went to churches or synagogues with names like First Presbyterian, Christ Episcopal, or Beth-Shalom. And we didn't.

White families vacationed in the summer at the shore, in the mountains, and at state parks for weeks at a time. And we didn't.

White kids talked back to their parents. And we didn't.

Black families listened to the same kind of music. We shared a musical legacy nurtured by the rough-hewed sounds of work songs that were later transformed into the blues. The haunting sounds of Negro spirituals seeped into contemporary gospel. Music resonated throughout the house every single day. The Jive Five, Little Anthony and the Imperials, and the Platters gave us doo-wop, and the Drifters serenaded us with songs like "Under the Boardwalk." We were mesmerized by the music.

Then came the pulsating sound of Motown. The smooth synchronized moves of the Temptations, the Miracles, the Supremes, the Marvelettes, and the Four Tops captured our imaginations. We all sang the chorus to "Say It Loud . . . I'm Black and I'm Proud!" as the James Brown anthem helped to galvanize a movement.

We had just entered junior high, senior high, or college when rhythm and blues took hold of the nation. The sensual sounds of Marvin Gaye, Barry White, Issac Hayes, and Luther Vandross were emotionally titillating. We added a heavy dosage of funk and danced to the music of Bloodstone; Earth, Wind, and Fire; Frankie Beverly and Maze; and Rufus and Chaka Khan. We emerged as graduates of classic soul, or what Tom Joyner gleefully refers to as "the old school sound."

We ushered in the afro and ushered out the Jheri-curl. We went from colored to Negro, from Negro to black, from black to Afro and then to African American in our quest for self-determination. As a people, we had the right to name ourselves.

When all was said and done, some of us had discovered the ease, simplicity, and unity in being black folks: strong, assertive, self-righteous people connected to the struggle of black people all over the world. And those young sisters who were comfortable in their group identity had a head start on those who were left conflicted by their formative experiences.

RICKI: CONNECTED TO FAMILY AND COMMUNITY

Ricki, a tall, slender, dark-hued woman with strikingly keen features, has natural hair the color of henna and a demeanor that is both sweet and sensual. She has vivid memories of growing up in an era of tremendous social and economic change. Her voice is laced with gaiety and sadness.

"Some of my best and worst memories are as a child and young teen growing up during the era of the civil rights movement," she said. "My worst memories are the murders, lynchings, beatings, and bombings of blacks and whites who played a role in the fight for civil and voting rights. But I also recall how we joined our parents in marches demanding equal rights, and how we marched in silent memorials for those slain in the struggle."

Not all of her memories focus on the turbulence of the times. As a member of a military family, Ricki clocked more frequent travel miles before the age of eight than many of her adult neighbors who refused to leave the comforts of their own backyards.

"I'm a navy brat," she states rather proudly. "I was born at Oak Knoll Naval Hospital in Oakland, California, the first of three children. My parents met, courted, and later married in San Francisco sometime after the bombing of Pearl Harbor. My father was a native of Milo, Oklahoma. He was tall, black, and handsome—the strong and silent type. My mother was born in Little Rock, Arkansas, but raised in Denver, Colorado. She was short, petite, shapely, very intelligent, and a very outspoken woman." There is obvious delight in sharing these memories of her early life.

"My earliest memories are of us living on the navy base in San Diego. My brother and sister, two and then four years after me, were born there. I remember shopping at the commissary, going to the beach and to baseball games with Dad. On Sundays, our family would take long drives in our big brown Chevrolet. I remember this well because not every family had a car. And not everyone had a TV. Friends and neighbors would come to our house to watch television."

Ricki watched *Howdy Doody with Buffalo Bob* and the early morning news shows. But there was more to life than watching television. Ricki fondly recalls her early school experience. What stands out the most is her first black teacher, Miss Emma. She taught Ricki the importance of education "and learning how to phonetically sound out each word in my first-grade reader that would open up the mysteries of Dick and Jane on Cherry Street."

Ricki's parents exposed her to dance, theater, and cultural events. Most important, they found ways to protect their children from the severe forms of racial segregation that were part of almost every black family's life and part of the military experience.

"My dad was a chief petty officer in the navy," Ricki said. "My family moved to a number of navy bases—first to Denver, Colorado, then Millington, Tennessee, and then Kansas City, Kansas. As we three kids got older, we would balk when it came time for the move to his next base assignment. I realize now that many times our family was given the assignment to be the first black family on the navy base. I remember my dad being on extra alert as he drove his precious family to his next duty station. Even though we lived in states where segregation and Jim Crow existed, as children we were spared the awful details. It was a long time before I understood why Daddy always went into the restaurant by himself before coming back to the car to wake us up to go in to breakfast—or, in some cases, drive on to a 'nicer' restaurant. It was even longer before I understood that not every family was forced to travel America's spacious highways with a *big* gun hidden up under the seat on the driver's side. And I always thought it was my mom's budget consciousness that kept us from staying in the big flashy hotels we passed by on our way to smaller hotels where most of the clientele was black like us. It was those big, grand, flashy places that I yearned to stay in. I vowed that I would stay in the best hotels money could buy one day."

There was a price to pay for being the first black to push forward in the military hierarchy. During the 1950s, promotion to rank in any branch of the military was viewed as a major achievement for a Negro. The entire community shared its pride in the individual's accomplishments. However, frequent moves by the family disrupted the children's sense of stability. A family needed to put down roots somewhere. With that in

mind, Ricki's parents relocated to the San Francisco area, settling into a middle-class community just outside the city.
According to Ricki, it was not exactly a move based on freedom of choice.

"In the late 1950s, my parents bought a house in the community of East Palo Alto near Stanford University in Palo
Alto. I say they 'bought,' but in reality they were redlined into
this community. White realtors refused to show or sell blacks
nicer homes in other areas that they could have afforded. Still,
being in such close proximity to Stanford was important to my
parents. They reasoned that racism was a function of ignorance, and that by living close to one of the nation's foremost
centers of learning they and their children would be subjected
to less ignorance, racism, and discrimination. They also hoped
exposure to the Stanford campus and its public programs
would give their children an educational incentive." Ricki
described what it was like to move into an integrated community.

"East Palo Alto was a racially mixed community when my
parents first bought their home. However, after a few years of
redlining, most of the residents were black. Still, it was a wonderful community of blacks trying to build a better life. The
East Palo Alto I grew up in was filled with fathers who went off
to work in the morning and mothers who stayed home caring
for their children."

In the summer, the kids were shipped off to Milo, Okla-
homa, to visit their grandparents and other extended family
members. Here they enjoyed home-cooked meals of "ham,
eggs, bacon, fish, grits, biscuits, toast, fried chicken, potatoes,

and homemade preserves which were grown, cured, or pro-duced on my grandparents' little farm." This was also a time for intergenerational sharing. Revitalizing an ancient African tradi-tion, the elders passed on the oral history in the form of story-telling. Their focus was always on the ancestors, a long line of strong, fiercely independent family members who feared no one. They protected their property with the aid of a gun and stood defiantly in the presence of white folks. And they were proud of their mixed heritage: descendants of Africans who joined forces with Florida's Black Seminole Indians to fight against white supremacy during the early period of conquest.

Ricki's family celebrated their black beauty long before it became vogue. This reinforced her sense of worth and self-esteem.

"Returning to East Palo Alto from those summers in Okla-homa, I was more proud of who I was," she said. "By the time I was in junior high school, I was angry about the way Negroes were misrepresented in the news media. What I read in news-paper stories and saw on TV was not my reality, and I vowed that I would one day be a TV reporter who would tell our side of the story." Thus, a seed was planted. Ricki envisioned a bright future on a pathway strongly marked by her career and her pos-itive, assertive identification with her people.

TEA: HUNGRY FOR FAME AND FORTUNE

Tea lived on the other side of Ricki's world. Born in 1948 near the port town of Norfolk, Virginia, Tea comes from a family that has resided in this community for four generations. The Dockins were not a military family, but they always seemed to have a relationship with the sea. The Norfolk area was a busy seaport and jobs were plentiful for men and women. Tea recalls a life of social sacrifice and personal privilege. Her mother, a short, stout woman with brown eyes and long wavy hair, was a domestic who alternated her time between working for white folks and tending to the needs of her family of five. Domestic service was exhausting work, and Tea remembers her mother always looking tired and complaining about the demands of her several employers.

"I remember her coming home late at night, telling one of us kids to get the pan and the Epsom salts so that she could soak her feet," Tea said. "We couldn't really talk to her until the ritual was completed." Tea's father, a medium-sized brown man with lots of hair on his face and chest, worked as a welder in a shipyard, or so she thought. "He used to say that he was a welder, but when I think about how poor we were and how little insurance money we got following his death, I don't think he was a welder at all. He may have been some kind of apprentice, but not a welder."

Tea was the family's entertainer and she took every opportunity available to show off her creativity when the family gathered. It gave her special status and privilege, and no one encouraged her more than her father. He would coax her to act, sing, dance, and play the piano to help develop her skills.

The emotionally stirring sounds of such great black jazz singers as Billie Holiday, Sarah Vaughn, and Nat King Cole were a staple in Tea's home. Then the old classic voices gave way to the new as the entire family danced and sang to the popular hits of Fats Domino, Chuck Berry, the Platters, the Shirells, and Little Richard on the new high-fidelity record player. However, nothing excited Tea's imagination more than the sensational rise to fame of teenage heartthrob Frankie Lymon. She was in love with him. Tea dreamed about growing up and becoming a famous rhythm and blues singer. She would be rich and famous and make her family proud. For Tea, money and fame were synonymous. She was totally unaware of the social and economic hardships faced by black entertainers.

Nevertheless, Tea's mind was set on a performing career. After school and on weekends, she practiced being "famous." In between rehearsals she played jacks, hopscotch, and hide-and-seek. She roller-skated, rode her bike, and enjoyed other outdoor activities. And she cherished the time she spent with her grandmother, aunts, and cousins who lived close by. With the little free time she had left, Tea watched the *Flintstones* on Friday night, but bypassed the Saturday morning cartoon extravaganza. She fondly recalls the excitement of seeing the Jackson Five on the *Ed Sullivan Show* and fell in love with Leslie Uggams on the *Lawrence Welk Show*, thinking that with any luck, she, too, might end up a star.

TERRI: STRUGGLING TO BELONG

Terri is also a daughter of the South. She was born in 1952 in a small community near Huntsville, Alabama. She describes her family as "dirt poor," barely able to survive. Her parents were always out and about searching for a better life. They were never capable of providing a stable home for their three children. Terri's maternal grandparents assumed the responsibility as the primary caretakers.

"Pop Pop bought land in the 1920s when everybody was struggling to make it. He built this house and raised my mother and my aunts and uncles here. This is the same house that me and my brothers and sisters were raised in, and now me and my four children and husband live here."

Terri's childhood was unremarkable. She climbed trees, swam in muddy holes, and played kickball on dirt roads. She does not remember watching television.

"I think I was ten years old before we got a TV in our house. It wasn't for us. That set was Pop Pop's pride and joy. I never really wanted to be bothered."

Terri was a voracious reader and enjoyed looking through magazines, admiring the people and surroundings projected from their glossy covers. During very private moments, she often wondered about her future. What would she look like? How would she live? Who would she marry? She found her answers inside the covers of black magazines like *Ebony*, *Jet*, and *Sepia*.

"*Ebony* and *Jet* were two magazines that were always lying around on the coffee table at my house," she recalls gleefully. "I would flip through the pages every month, looking for pictures of famous black people. I used to see pictures of movie stars, singers, preachers, and pretty light-skinned women and good-looking men with curly hair. That's where I wanted to be."

Looking at pictures in black magazines provided young black girls with positive images of the community. Projecting glamorous images of cute little light-skinned people with curly hair could be viewed as a real plus. However, by the mid-1960s, blacks were questioning the portrayal of African Americans in the media. And *Ebony* and *Jet* were not immune from the attacks.

In February 1966, when Terri was just fifteen years old, *Ebony*'s cover story raised the question, "Are Negro Girls Getting Prettier?" A storm of controversy followed. Critics charged that the photos of *Ebony*'s pretty Negro girls were light-skinned black women with Caucasian features. Were black women of a darker hue with short kinky hair less attractive? How long would the community remain fixated on the belief that the standard of beauty was measured by light skin, long stringy hair, and thin lips?

Black people have always struggled with the issue of color. It is an old festering wound slow to heal and difficult to tackle. *Ebony*'s article focused renewed attention on a sensitive subject that most blacks preferred to keep within the confines of the black community. Much like racism, colorism is a distinct social disorder that assigns higher social value to those with lighter skin tones. It, too, is based on the false assumption that those with lighter skin possess superior and more desirable social and physical characteristics. It's not surprising that Terri and other young girls like her would see this image as desirable.

Terri attended a Catholic school for black children where lessons of faith, honesty, and hard work were instilled with an iron fist. She recalls an extremely disciplined environment where nuns possessed unquestionable authority. After six years, she left the Catholic school and was bused to the public school where black students were forced to attend. Terri describes her introduction to public school as one of "cultural shock."

"I had never been in a setting where everything was so uncontrollable," she confessed. "Kids had fights, threw spitballs, and talked back to the teachers. It was very chaotic." Terri was an excellent student, having acquired good study habits during her tenure in the Catholic school system. It was her grandparents, who had been such a stable influence throughout her childhood, who prepared Terri for college. They had high aspirations for their granddaughter. Terri recalls them saying, "Negroes can be anything they want to be now. 'Twasn't like that before, but 'tis now." Becoming a schoolteacher was held in high esteem as a career choice. If she set her sights high, she could make it. But Terri wanted to be a pharmacist. Following high school graduation, she was off to attend Spelman, a historical black college in Atlanta, Georgia. It was her first and only choice. Terri would have many career options to pursue. But first she had to find one of those cute curly-headed boys.

CHRYSTAL: SEEKING THE ELUSIVE OPPORTUNITY TO BE SOMEBODY

Forty-five-year-old Chrystal grew up farther north where free blacks had planted roots in communities such as Philadelphia, Boston, and New York more than two hundred years earlier. A mass migration flooded the areas before and after World Wars I and II. Black folks have always believed that the North held the greatest promise for freedom and social opportunities. Life was better, but not equal. In Chrystal's case, her family was among the first generation of blacks to live in the Newark, New Jersey, area.

Chrystal was born into a stable working-class family. She is the second of five children born to Sharon and Raymond Alexander. All of the siblings share membership in the baby-boom generation. Chrystal recalls her father as a hardworking gentleman who was an excellent provider. A lifelong worker for U.S. Steel, his job as a boilermaker kept the family in relative comfort in their modest three-bedroom row home west of the city's center. Free of most vices, Chrystal describes her father as a good husband—"always willing to bring home the bacon"—to a strong-willed, domineering woman who served as the family disciplinarian. A slight man with a red-brown hue, chain-smoking was his only indulgence.

Images of Chrystal's mother are decidedly different. A churchgoing Catholic, Mrs. Alexander juggled her time between working as a nurse's aide and raising a family. The family was the most important focus of her life. Trying to provide extra comforts to her five children in a stifling urban environment meant working part-time to save up a little "pin money" for family emergencies. She was as representative as any strong black woman who performed Herculean tasks with limited social resources for family, friends, and community.

Chrystal, like many her age, watched Mickey Mouse, played with her Betsy Wetsy doll, and perfected her double Dutch skills when weather permitted. She was aware of the issues surrounding race long before she struggled with the issue of color.

"I lived in a mixed neighborhood," she recalls. "Well, first it was mixed and then it was black. I remember the elementary school being mostly black kids. Junior and senior high schools were mixed with black and white students, but mainly Italians. That's when I first noticed that white kids were different. White kids were in special classes, liked by the teachers, and always seemed to be in control of student government. Black kids didn't have those kind of advantages." As she continues to relate her story, Chrystal recalls her own involvement with extracurricular activities. "I remember joining the marching band. I wanted to be somebody special. Seeing all those people march around in blue and red uniforms was so impressive. I couldn't wait for my mother to see me marching down the field."

The opportunity to be somebody came at the annual Thanksgiving Day home football game that pitted the school against its favorite crosstown rival. It was a longstanding tradition attended by generations of family members. For the Alexanders, it was a family affair.

"After the game was over, I went running to the bleachers to meet my mother. As a child, you have such a need to be validated by your parents. I remember the only person I thought about when I was marching out on that field was my mother. 'Chrystal, you looked pretty good out there for a dark girl' was what she said to me. It still stands out in my mind until this day. Why did she have to emphasize 'for a dark girl'?" From that moment on, color and colorism joined race and racism. Before long, Chrystal began to feel the social restrictions placed on dark-skinned black girls.

Chrystal worked hard to get through high school, where academics were not stressed as the priority for black students. Many had been tracked into less challenging curriculums in the trade and clerical areas. Students were being prepared for jobs, not higher education. Most of her black classmates graduated high school and secured low-paying jobs, but Chrystal wanted to do more.

"I wanted to go to college when I graduated," she said, "but I remember being told that I wasn't smart enough. We [girls] were advised not to go into degree programs. Nursing, secretarial, or beauty school were the three main choices. I went to secretarial school. I guess I was planning on being a receptionist or something like that. When I was about to graduate from the program, it was clear to me that all the other girls, who were all white, were engaged to be married. I wanted to get married, too. I pressured my boyfriend into giving me a ring and setting a wedding date. I was doing what everybody else was doing. At the time, I thought it was the right thing to do." Chrystal is pensive, almost melancholy, as she reflects on these early memories.

"The school was planning a special ceremony for the graduation. We had been given special instructions on how to look like a business professional. The right suit, the right color, and the right hairstyle. I wore my hair in an Afro. I remember that there was a lot of discussion among the instructors about who would approach me and tell me to change my hair—straighten it to make it more presentable. I dared them to make a move. I had lost so much of my self-esteem being surrounded by all of these white women. I wasn't about to give up my newly found identity."

Chrystal marched down the aisle in her queen-sized Afro, looking much like Angela Davis. She has never regretted her decision to take a stand. Six weeks later, she put on a white Victorian wedding dress, straightened her hair, and exchanged vows in a traditional Catholic ceremony. On that special day, the pressure to conform to tradition superseded Chrystal's need to flaunt her new sense of cultural identity.

SHELLI: SURVIVING SHATTERED DREAMS

Shelli's family also relocated from the South to the North. Shelli was raised in a small community outside of Columbus, Ohio. It was an old, settled community where people maintained strong connections to their Southern heritage. She recalls a lifetime of love and security, comforted by the knowledge that she belonged to somebody—in fact, several somebodies. "It was a small, very countrified black community," Shelli states. "There were no sidewalks, no fire or police departments. Everything was volunteer. It was very family oriented. If the person across the street saw you do something wrong, you were in trouble just like if your parents saw you do something wrong. Everybody looked out for everybody else."

Everybody in the community worked. Her mother was employed as a clerk in a tool and die company. It was hard work with low pay. Her father earned a living as a construction worker. Time was spent romping up and down the neighbor-hood, engaging in all the activities that girls were not supposed to do. Every summer, Shelli and her sister were banished to her aunt Sadie's farm in Clayton, South Carolina, where they acquired lessons in farming, family responsibility, and caring. Shelli's brother, six years her senior, was always allowed to remain in the city.

Shelli never gave much thought to being black. It was obvious. Over the years, Shelli's family had remained close to their African roots, and her daily struggle with her tightly curled, coarse hair and bush comb reinforced her connection to a community of dark-skinned people who looked very much like herself. The family enjoyed a close bond. Throughout much of her young life, Shelli was embraced by loving parents and two older siblings who she adored. She was stunned when her father announced that he was leaving the home, and he was taking his son with him. At sixteen years of age, Shelli found the situation unbearable and couldn't imagine how she would continue to lead a normal life.

For a brief time, her schoolwork suffered, which caused her parents much concern. They both wanted their daughter to succeed. It would increase her chances of going to college and getting a good job at one of the big companies in the downtown area. Shelli's parents often talked about college, but didn't prepare for it financially. She dreamed of going to Howard University, a historical black college in Washington, D.C. As she discussed her plans with her parents, who now occupied two separate households, she realized that she was too poor to leave home. Her dreams shattered, Shelli began to think about employment opportunities in the retail market. However, upon graduation from high school, Shelli did not seek employment. Instead, she enrolled in a summer enrichment program targeted at minority students, and, in 1977, became the first member of her family to enter college at the state university. Word of her acceptance spread like wildfire throughout the community. It was a time for rejoicing.

JUDITH: THE CONTRADICTIONS OF COLOR AND CLASS

Judith remembers a time when the whole world seemed to be her playground. Born in 1955 in a resort community that was home to many upper-class white families wanting to escape from the inner cities during the summer season, Judith's view of the ocean, coupled with the gentle aroma of salted sea water, created an environment conducive to fanciful dreams. Judith's parents, early entrepreneurs who established a successful mom-and-pop grocery store in the neighborhood where blacks lived, were able to create a comfortable home for the family. Her mother and father doted on her and her seven siblings. There never seemed to be any doubt that she would find a satisfying life.

At an early age, Judith was exposed to life's contradictions. Her family was much admired for their ability to live comfortably as a middle-class black family, but they were always reminded of their second-class status when the community was flooded with wealthy white tourists in the summer. While legal segregation did not exist, de facto segregation was evident. All the black families lived in one part of town. They were seasonal employees, fulfilling service-oriented jobs during the high season and collecting unemployment in the off-peak.

Judith was aware of the discrepancies between the black and white worlds but always felt proud of her heritage. Her parents supplemented their education with black history lessons and limited their exposure to negative images on television, in books, and in other media. She has early memories of her father, Samuel, planning a career for each child—one that he felt was suited to his or her unique personality and ability. Judith's anticipated role was that of a physician. Her father lectured his children on the need to work extra hard and warned them about the racist nature of American society. White people, who he disparaged frequently, were not to be trusted.

Judith was a seventh-grade student at the only junior high in the city when she got her first real lesson on the far-reaching effects of racial polarity in America.

"I can't quite remember what started the fight, but it was some struggle between me and another female student. As she walked away from me, she turned around and called me a mulatto. I didn't know what that was, but I was smart enough to go look it up in the dictionary. When I saw the definition, I knew that she didn't know what she was talking about. A mulatto was the child of a white and black person. I went home and told my mother about the incident. She looked at me and said, 'Yeah. That's what you are.' That's when she told me that my father was white—in fact, a German. I was shocked—in a state of total disbelief. It never occurred to me that my father was white. He didn't even like white people. As a family, we were always black. I thought my father was a light-skinned man with dark crinkled hair." Judith's mother used the opportunity to explain her past, which she had never wanted to discuss with the children.

Samuel Smith was born in Germany in 1897. His family immigrated to the United States in the early 1900s. He was schooled in the ways of America, his new country: freedom, democracy, fair competition, and the opportunity to achieve life, liberty, and the pursuit of happiness. Lessons promoting racial supremacy were undoubtedly included as part of his indoctrination process. His family settled in Georgia, one of the most segregated states in the Union. Samuel heeded his father's directions, taking advantage of free education, committing himself to hard work, and maintaining a strong dedication to family above all else. He and his two brothers formed an import/export business that specialized in antiques trading. It became a tremendous success. Samuel had made it. One generation removed from the Old World, this hardworking German American family had captured the American dream. However, during his business travels to Virginia he encountered Sally Mae, a black woman, and fell deeply in love.

Sally Mae was a tall, slender woman with honey brown skin. She was pleasant to look at and enjoyed the comforts of a loving but very poor family. She was the third child born into a family whose southern roots ran deep. However, her greatest quality was that of being a decent, caring human being. Samuel was twenty-five years older than Sally Mae—an issue that was of much concern to her mother—and he was white. It was an unlikely coupling. Convinced that he had found the love of his life, Samuel proposed marriage. That's when their real troubles began.

In Virginia, it was illegal for whites to marry blacks or any other person of color. Undaunted, Samuel continued to confess his love for Sally Mae, eventually persuading her to leave the South to move to New England, where laws prohibiting interracial marriage did not exist. They traveled along the eastern shore, stopping to get married in a small chapel in Pennsylvania. However, they stumbled across a small resort town during a brief rest period. Fascinated by the view of the ocean and the endless supply of fresh air, Sally Mae and Samuel altered their plans and took up residence in the community. They never left.

Samuel expected to continue his successful work in the family business. During the week, he traveled to old estate homes in the southern part of the country seeking priceless antiques. He had mastered his craft and there was very little doubt that he was the expert in the family. However, Samuel's family vehemently objected to his marriage to a Negro. Judith and her children were not welcome in the family home. And after years of struggle, Samuel was not only forced out of the business but also cheated out of his fair share of the profits and inheritance.

Samuel had no other choice but to begin anew. He and Sally Mae established their own business, continued to have children, and enjoyed a passionate relationship until the very end. Samuel died in 1967 at the age of sixty-nine. It was only a few short months after Judith discovered that her father was a white man. Judith reminisces: "It's one of those things that eventually you accept as true, but you're always searching for ways to explain why it happened."

Judith's parents' decision to hide her father's true racial identity was puzzling to her. Within the black community, there is a long documented history of people of African descent trying to escape their identity by "passing." However, much less attention has been focused on the small population of individuals who for whatever reasons decide to leave their privileged status as white Americans and choose to live their lives as members of the African American community. I refer to this practice as *shading*.

Shading has never been a popular practice in America, although there are some documented cases where people have confessed to perpetrating fraud in regard to their racial identity. In James McBride's bestselling book, *The Color of Water* (1997), he discussed how his white Jewish mother spent most of her life posing as a black woman in a Brooklyn housing project. Having married a black man and being the mother of twelve black children, denying her European heritage may have been the easiest way to cope in a racially charged environment. Shading permitted her to do just that.

The practice of shading is far more extreme than the mere art of imitation. For years, members of the white community have imitated black culture for profit and entertainment. Elvis duplicated the moves of Chuck Berry; the Osmonds were a carbon copy of the Jackson Five; and 'N Sync, the Backstreet Boys, and Eminem have exploited black culture to the point where their efforts are currently being described as a new form of "white soul." Moreover, shading differs significantly from the vicarious experience that suburban white youth are having with hip-hop culture. Efforts to act, speak, dress, and move like members of the black community have earned these teens the derogatory title of "whiggers"—a term used by their black inner city counterparts.

However, Judith's father was a true shader. He had given up his status as a privileged white male to live in harmony with his wife and children. He saw the value in black people, black culture, and the black community. But questions about his decision to conceal his racial identity from the children would go unanswered. Judith's father was gone. He left her with a powerful understanding of the tensions surrounding race and color. Race matters, and the color conflict persists.

Judith's desire to fulfill her father's dream raged on. She was to become a doctor. It was the career that her father had picked for her. Following her graduation from Mainland High School, she enrolled in an accelerated premed program that promised early admission to medical school after the completion of just three years of college.

DARLA: MIXED EMOTIONS

Darla's parents were from two different regions of the country. Her father's people were from New York City. Her mother's folks were from Jackson, Mississippi. They were a family of tenant farmers who grew cotton and tobacco and produced a large family to help take care of the farm. It was a difficult life, but the family eked out enough income to survive and care for all of their offspring. The events surrounding World War II would change their lives forever.

Darla's grandfather, Mr. Jefferson, was long past the age where compulsory wartime service could threaten his livelihood as a tenant farmer. He was not a military man and felt no need to be overly patriotic, but two of his sons were in the army. He understood the nation's wartime needs. When his eldest daughter, Edmona, asked permission to travel north to secure employment at a good-paying job, her wish was granted. There was one stipulation: She had to return home the way she left—no marriage, no kids, no trouble!

It was not difficult to secure employment during wartime, since it was a period of unprecedented job growth. Both black and white women were needed to fill jobs left vacant by the deployment of thousands of young men in the armed forces and to fill newly created jobs that resulted from the war.

Edmona was fortunate. She quickly landed a job at the Quartermasters station for the U.S. Army. There she met up with longtime city slicker Lucus Warren and before long fell deeply in love with the handsome copper-toned boy who constantly bragged about his credentials as a Morehouse man. Once the war ended, Lucus was offered a federal job with the Department of Civil Defense. It would necessitate a move to New Haven, Connecticut, where he hoped to set up house with Edmona. Recalling her pledge to her father, Edmona felt obligated to return home, primarily to demonstrate her willingness to fulfill her commitment to the family and to remain a positive role model for her younger sisters and brothers. Lucus thought only for a brief moment before he agreed to return south with Edmona to woo her father into agreeing that he was responsible enough to ask for Edmona's hand in marriage.

It took more than a year to work out all of the details, but Edmona and Lucus were married in 1947 and had their first child, Darla, in December 1950. (Edmona borrowed the name Darla from her favorite movie matinee idol on *The Little Rascals*.) Lucus, being an old-fashioned man, felt that a woman's place was in the home. Despite her desire to secure outside employment to supplement the household income, Lucus prohibited his wife from working.

Darla wanted to be a cowgirl. The Warrens shared their home with Edmona's second cousin and her young son, Junie, who was barely one year older than Darla. Both Junie and Darla enjoyed propping themselves before the television set to watch *Hop a Long Cassidy*, *Roy Rogers*, and other cowboy shows that were popular during the mid-1950s. *The Roy Rogers and Dale Evans Show* was her favorite. It stimulated the imagination. Her self-identity was being molded by a couple who encouraged young boys and girls like Darla and Junie to wave hello and goodbye to the television set as they greeted other kids from all over the nation.

Darla and Junie had been waving for several years, hoping to see their faces among the featured guests one Saturday morning. It never happened, and Darla wondered why. It was Junie, with all the wisdom and maturity of a seven-year-old, who revealed to Darla that people who looked like them would never be on *The Roy Rogers and Dale Evans Show*. "It's 'cause we're dis" were his exact words as he rubbed his finger up and down Darla's milk chocolate arm. It was her first exposure to racism, and the pain still lingers.

She never wanted to be a cowgirl after that. Relocation took the family west, from Sacramento to San Diego, and then to Portland, Oregon. Her mother got her ready for third grade and prepared her to assume a new role and a new identity.

"My mother gave me strict lessons. As she dressed me for the first day of school, she reminded me that I was a Negro. This, she said, would be the first time that many of these young children and their teachers had ever been exposed to a Negro. It was my job to be a good Negro, or what later on became an *exceptional* Negro, because I was representing my family, my community, and myself. Anything that I did would be a reflection on the entire Negro race. From the very beginning, I was raised to be an overachiever."

Darla was under pressure to perform. The weight of the race was placed squarely on her small shoulders. And it was a heavy burden. She shares the details of her story in an emotionally charged voice, as if she were acting out a major drama in a high school play.

"There was never more than a handful of blacks in each school that I entered. I always felt like an ugly duckling. I didn't wear the right clothes, I wore very thick glasses, and I looked terribly undernourished. I didn't know about makeup or how to do my hair because there were so few black girls to hang out with to try to work these things out.

"I was an extremely bright student, and that did work to my advantage. I remember my parents going to school on back-to-school night to meet with my teachers. They sat proudly in the classroom as Mrs. Riley talked about the students who were eligible for the National Honor Society, of which I was one. At the end of the presentation, my parents approached Mrs. Riley and asked her what she thought of me. She honestly answered that she didn't really know me because I was a nonverbal child who didn't participate in extracurricular activities.

"My parents came home fuming and blessed me out. I was to go back to school and make certain that I demonstrated my ability to be an exceptional Negro. And I did. I joined every club imaginable, ran for student government office, and rose to the top of my class. I maxed out on the SAT. It's almost embarrassing. My scores were so high that I had a choice to go to any school that I pleased. I returned back north to the University of Connecticut."

When Darla left home, she left behind more than her parents and three siblings. She left a childhood of mixed emotions where her struggle to achieve was always precariously balanced between what she wanted, who she wanted to be as an individual, and what she needed to do for her parents and the community.

She arrived on campus during a volatile period in the civil rights movement. Martin Luther King Jr. had been assassinated in April 1968, just two months before Darla's high school graduation. Black people no longer wanted to be called Negroes, and student unrest, coupled with the frustration surrounding the Vietnam War, was at its peak.

Darla was uncertain of who or what she wanted to be, but she was no longer willing to play the role of the exceptional

Negro. Darla the Negro was dead. And Darla began her search for a new, self-defined identity.

SISTER WISDOM

Several issues emerge from the shared childhood memories of these sisters. And, undoubtedly, questions about your own past have started to resurface. What stands out in your mind as some of the most memorable events of childhood? What were your dreams about the future? What media images helped you to shape an identity for yourself? How did you handle life's early successes and disappointments?

Reviewing the text of childhood memories can be an especially useful tool in helping African American women appreciate the array of factors that have played a significant role in their formative years. Piecing together the past opens the door to understanding what's meaningful to you as an individual now.

Concerns about race, color, identity, and just wanting to be somebody continued to dominate the experiences of these sisters for years to come. But I believe helpful lessons about these issues take root during the age of innocence. As girls who grew up to be self-affirming black women, Ricki, Tea, Chrystal, Shelli, Judith, Darla, and Terri learned the following:

- *Race and sex always matter, and the color complex endures.* Regardless of the region or residential setting, these sisters came away from childhood with a fine-tuned understanding of the meaning of race, color, and gender in the black community. Their perceptions of differential treatment for whites and blacks, for light and dark complexions, and for males and females helped to solidify their understanding of the many obstacles that they would encounter as young black women.

- *Life is unfair, and at times people are unkind.* No one else will love you like your parents. The unconditional love that was showered upon you in your formative years by parents, family, and community can provide you with the strength and fortitude needed to survive in hostile environments.
- *You must have high expectations for yourself if you want to succeed.* Pursuing a successful personal or career path was within the realm of possibility. Black parents who recognized that their opportunities were limited but saw tremendous potential for advancement in their offspring made every attempt to prepare them for a brighter future. These parents laid important groundwork for their daughters' future satisfaction.
- *Our community and culture count.* Black folks are a community of people with a unique culture and unique ways of viewing the world. Learning to respect and value the strengths of our own community is part of our heritage. Learning to view the world from a black cultural perspective is a tenet that we must pass down from generation to

generation. When little girls are taught to see themselves as the beneficiaries of the wisdom of their elders, they are protected for the rest of their lives from the worst psychological effects of negative images, messages, and experiences related to race and gender.

3

Great Expectations:

Discovering Who We Want to Be

In hindsight, it is easy to forget that young adulthood is a time of great uncertainty. Darla looked back on her young adult years as "the bestest of times." It was simply wonderful to be young. She had dreams, ambition, high energy, and an ethereal vision of how perfect her life was going to be. She looked good, felt great, and she was in the best physical shape ever. But trial-and-error can be rough. Test runs are emotionally draining and sometimes life-threatening. Launching professional and personal goals requires hard work. You need money, skills, plans, and a road map to realize dreams.

Some sisters make headway. Others do not. As one of the women I interviewed put it:

I often think about the dreams I once had as a young woman. Who doesn't think about finding the right partner, settling down, having a few kids, and finding a good place to live? I mean, I wasn't exactly looking for the white knight in shining armor 'cause Cinderella doesn't look like me. But I did hope for a better life than what I'm experiencing right now. I never expected to be a single parent, never thought I'd have to deal with domestic violence, and was fairly certain that black people would be a lot further along than they are right now.

—*Theresa, age 41*

Although our dreams begin in childhood, the quest to fulfill them begins in earnest following graduation from high school or college. Young sisters desire many things. Some do want to live like the princess at the end of the perfect storybook tale. Some want freedom, having the ability to do what they please, when they please, and how they please. Others seek careers in traditional professions such as teaching, nursing, civil service, or social work. Still others choose to pursue careers in new fields that are opening up in government and in corporate America.

Sisters who are midlifers were born into a rapidly changing, technologically advanced society. The value of a high school diploma decreased sharply, and more and more students felt the need to pursue additional educational and training opportunities in order to secure good-paying jobs. It was generally anticipated that a surge in attendance of black students at the nation's institutions of higher education would prove beneficial to the entire community.

Many of us pioneered in our career choices. But I think it is fair to say that few of us expected to be pioneers in our personal lives as well. Like most women in every generation before and after us, we were also seeking lovers, boyfriends, husbands—someone special to love and be loved by.

TEA'S SEARCH

Tea began her search for the good life with a painfully unrealistic view of the world. In the comforts of a loving, supportive, all-black environment, she was a budding star and the darling of her daddy's eye. But her education had not prepared her for the stiff competition and rejection that she would face immediately after high school. To this day, she remains angry at the betrayal.

"Throughout my life I loved school," she said. "But black children in that school were not destined to go anywhere. I knew about racism, but I didn't have the power to do anything about it. I didn't have the tools, didn't have the skills. Our parents couldn't do anything, either. I saw the difference between black kids and white kids, and knew that white kids were always selected to be at the top of everything.

"The teachers were racist—even the ones who treated us quite fairly were all racist. Our parents couldn't do anything, but teachers knew the difference between right and wrong." In vain, Tea tried her best to overcome the limits placed on her by her environment.

"I wanted so badly to be perfect. I would do things for the teachers to gain their favor. I devised a strategy to earn brownie points with my teachers. I would never get to the top, but I worked my way up as far as I could. That was the game and that was the way I was going to play it.

"It's quite sad when you think about it—all the things a black child had to do to get some recognition. I remember talking about my career goals during career week and how the teachers responded to me. 'That's all well and good,' they said. 'But you need a job.' I left school on a Friday. Monday was a holiday. On Tuesday I was working in a factory."

The world was changing for black people and Tea knew it. However, she was not on her way to college as she had hoped, but had started her post–high school working career in a dead-end factory job filled with struggling, uneducated, underpaid black and white women.

"I knew that I didn't want to be there, but I had to be there anyway. There was something more that I wanted to do. I wanted to take control of my life, but I didn't know how. Again, I didn't have the skills or the tools to help me determine what had gone wrong. When you're in a factory, you sit there and do your work. You never speak out of turn. You never go on break until it's time, and you ask permission to go to the toilet. I was new to the job, but other women had been there for years and years. The supervisor was rude, ignorant to all of the workers. Everyone was fearful and never talked back to her.

"One day I saw her bullying some poor young white girl. She wouldn't defend herself, but I did. The supervisor looked at me and said, 'How dare you speak to me like that!' She sent me to the head boss, expecting me to get fired. I gave him a piece of my mind, too. Instead of firing me, he asked me if I wished to work with the supervisor on the sewing machines. I told him no, and he sent me to a new job in the stockroom.

"Everybody thought that I was going to come back into the sewing area, pick up my coat, and very sheepishly walk out of the factory. Instead, I lifted my coat from the machine and announced that I had just been promoted to the stockroom."

Tea's reality didn't match her vision for the future. She wanted to have a meaningful life, and factory work would not provide it. It was the kind of dispiriting, harsh, drudging existence that helped you to focus on your future goals in a hurry.

Shelli, a black woman ten years Tea's junior and living in the more progressive North in Ohio, told me a similar story that happened to her a decade later.

"After my first year of college, I wasn't certain that I wanted to go back to school," Shelli said. "A lot of kids got started and never finished, and I didn't think that there was any particular shame in that. My mother got me a job working with her in the factory, and it didn't take long for me to get used to the money.

"The work environment was horrible. You would have to stand up all day and sort some funny little parts. I'm five foot one and my mother was an inch or two shorter than me. I remember this little Jewish guy, no bigger than the both of us, standing over us yelling and screaming about getting our work done. You couldn't make a move without somebody's permission. How could they make a grown woman ask for permission to pee?

"I worked in the factory all summer because I needed the money. What frightened me the most was the realization that my mother and other women just like her had spent their entire lives working under these horrid conditions. After that experience, I never doubted the value of higher education. I couldn't wait to get back to school and continue my studies."

Getting away from the factory became Tea's primary goal. A goal, she had learned, was different from a dream. As she reflected on earlier dreams of her life as an entertainer, she knew that something had gone horribly wrong.

"As a young girl I was into make-believe. I could sing, I could dance, and I could play the piano. My whole family was into that. I saw pictures of Judy Garland singing, cut out photos of black entertainers from the black magazines, and hung up posters of famous people. I knew there was something out there for me. I had a supportive family: my mom, my dad, and my aunties. But they didn't have the knowledge to point me in the right direction. They were there for me, right on the doorstep. However, racism was right on the doorstep, too. I think this is when I first became aware of institutional racism because so many black people were in the same situation as me."

Before long, Tea was able to convert her dream of going to college into a realistic goal. She left the factory after six months in search of an office job. She encountered more racism and challenges to her skills, but this time she was better prepared. She recalls being tested for a clerical position and the expression of disbelief on the examiner's face when she passed the test.

Tea's entrance into college was delayed by several years, but finally she was admitted to Hampton University. Once she arrived, she was committed to doing the very best that she could in order to turn her life around. As a young woman still in her early twenties, she felt that she had a lot of catching up to do. The important thing was that Tea had not given up. She had gotten herself back on track.

Hampton University is a historically black college in Virginia founded in 1868 during the period of Reconstruction. It enjoys a reputation as one of the finest black schools in the nation, and is often jokingly referred to as the "Harvard of the East" for black students. Steeped in tradition, ritual, and cultural nuances, sororities and fraternities are an integral part of college life: Deltas, AKAs, Zetas, Omegas, Kappas, Sigmas and Alphas all have a special place on the campus. In this idyllic, bucolic setting, friendships were forged, marriage partners found, cultural bonds solidified, and fond memories created that would last for a lifetime. Students who attended Hampton and other historically black colleges in the 1960s and 1970s had a much greater chance of graduating and receiving their bachelor's degrees than black students who attended predominantly white colleges.

There are plenty of sisters at Hampton, always disproportionate to the number of men. This is true for many of the historically black institutions, including Fisk University, North Carolina Central University, Morgan State University, Virginia State College, Cheney State University, Howard University, and Wilberforce University. It is generally agreed that the competition for male mates is always stiff.

Carla, who like Tea was at Hampton in the late sixties and early seventies, mused about the carefully orchestrated system of social dating that operated in full force while she was there.

"When you first arrived on campus, you were swarmed by the upperclassmen," Carla said. "It was open season on the freshmen. You still have plenty of dating opportunities as you reached your sophomore year, but there was a theory of diminishing returns. By the time you became a junior or senior, you were completely out of the loop."

Yet Carla remained certain that being at Hampton was the smartest choice she ever made. She is firm in her belief that nothing else compares to the black college experience, which included rigorous academic training. When the time came to prepare for her oral examinations for her doctorate degree, she had no doubt that her solid educational foundation was nurtured and developed at Hampton.

Tea, who was older than most of her classmates at Hampton, was not as interested in the dating game. She wanted to get her degree, start a career in the performing arts, and move away from the South. At Hampton, she nurtured her love for the arts and continued to use every opportunity to fine-tune her performance skills. And for the first time in her life, she envisioned a role for herself that went beyond the socially constrictive confines of the South. After she completed her studies, she headed to New York and the bright lights of the Great White Way.

Her move to the Big Apple was not difficult. A kinder, gentler theater environment greeted Tea and other talented young black artists in the 1970s than black performers experience today. Black productions were in vogue. The Negro Ensemble Company had successfully produced *The River Niger. Don't Bother Me, I Can't Cope* was the award-winning best musical for 1972. Blacks had starring roles in *Hair*, *The Wiz*, and *Golden Boy*. Talent was abundant, but opportunity was available. However, Tea was sidetracked by marriage and the birth of her son. At the age of twenty-five, Tea put her Broadway dreams on hold.

Once again, the path to her idealized vision of the future had taken a twist. But it was undeniable that Tea had shown courage and made significant headway.

TERRI'S SEARCH

Terri never gave any thought to leaving the South. The temperatures were mild, the people were friendly, and she needed to stay close to home to check on her grandparents. Terri was from a small town and, for the most part, lived a sheltered life. Being in the city of Atlanta marked the beginning of her worldly existence. She started her course work at Spelman College, took advantage of the city's nightlife, and began the search for a cute curly-headed boy. When Terri begins to reflect on her young adult years, her conversation slows as she ponders her response to each question.

"I got turned on to a lot of things in the city. College life was wonderful. I was enrolled at one of the most prestigious institutions in the south. I was a liberated adolescent with the freedom to do anything I wanted. I had plenty of opportunity to date boys my age and saw the possibility of making lifelong friendships. It was also a period in my life when I began to experiment with drugs.

"I started having a serious relationship with one of the football players from a neighboring school. I thought I was in love, so we moved in together and married shortly thereafter. We did the drug thing together. It wasn't long after that when school seemed to get in the way of the things that I wanted to do. After two years of college, I quit and went looking for a job. The local police department was doing a heavy recruitment campaign, focusing on the need for blacks and women to join the department. I was both. I entered the academy when I was twenty-one years old." Terri appeared hesitant to continue with the rest of her story. In encouraging her to be forthcoming, I again assured her of the confidential nature of her responses and coaxed her into describing the experiences of a young sister seeking a career in law enforcement.

"In many ways, it was the worst decision of my life, especially as a black woman. But it did open my eyes to many things. It was difficult to separate the good from the bad. The police officers that I worked with were very sick people. There was more corruption inside the department than outside. And while I stayed on the force for seven years, I never did give up my drug use." Terri was a polydrug abuser; amphetamines, marijuana, alcohol, and cocaine were her drugs of choice.

Persistent drug abuse was just one of Terri's problems. Her stormy marriage to the football player ended in separation after two years. She was having an affair with another member of the team and, for a brief period, continued the relationship after her marriage was over. Free, black, and twenty-one, Terri pursued the hedonistic lifestyle with a vengeance. She moved in and out of relationships, perhaps too frequently. She had three abortions. At the age of twenty-eight, when she became pregnant for the fourth time, Terri decided to carry the baby to full term. She was involved with a fellow officer, an "average run-of-the-mill white boy." The relationship had ended months before she discovered her pregnancy.

"He was single and available. I think he wanted to do the right thing. He seemed to have strong feelings about my carrying his child. He proposed marriage, but I was not interested. I couldn't see myself making a lifetime commitment to this man. We didn't share enough in common to share a life together. Sex and drugs are two different things. I mean white is white and black is black. Corned beef and cabbage is not black-eyed peas and rice."

Terri went out on maternity leave and never returned to the force. She was out of the policing business and considered what other options might be available to her. She had not completed college and had not prepared herself for a career change. While low-wage jobs were readily available, the weekly salary would not cover the cost of living. In addition to rent, food, transportation, and utility expenses, Terri was concerned about the exorbitant costs of child care.

She had been a member of this stable working-class black community for nearly a decade, but her social supports were limited. At the age of twenty-nine, she was a new mother with an infant son and nowhere to turn for assistance. Uncertain of what the future held, she packed her belongings and returned to her grandparents' home in Alabama.

RICKI'S SEARCH

When Ricki graduated from high school in 1966 and set her sights on college, her vision of who and what she wanted to be was crystal clear. Television continued to be a major influence. She admired the work of NBC's morning newscaster Dave Garroway from the time she was a little girl and thought she could be just like him. She was angry about the racial injustices leveled against the African American community and was willing to fight for social change. Broadcast journalism would be her weapon of choice. Ricki dreamed of taking to the airwaves to educate, inform, and ultimately transform the nation's image of black America.

Stanford University was close to home. Ricki's parents' strong belief that locating the family near an educational institution would help foster a love of education and a greater familiarity with the benefits of higher education in their offspring bore fruit. However, their dream that education would help to wipe out prejudice and ignorance in their lifetime remained barren. Ricki took advantage of the special enrichment programs that Stanford offered to local junior and senior high school students. She discovered that she was just as smart and just as capable as any rich white student, but Ricki was also reminded that as a black student she would have to be two to three times better if she wanted to make her mark in the world.

A strong academic program at Ravenswood High School prepared Ricki for the competitive world of college. She was convinced that she could make it through the academically rigorous curriculum of Stanford University, but Stanford was not her choice. Ricki needed to strike out on her own, and commuting back and forth to the local university was not too appealing. Besides, she was a traveling woman enthralled with the possibility of exploring vast territories in other parts of the country.

Ricki considered attending a college hundreds of miles away from home, but not before her parents were assured that there would be folks in the neighborhood to take care of their child. Black parents instinctively knew not to drop off their children in unfamiliar territory where there was no one around to nurture, guide, cook hot meals, and provide a safe haven far away from home. This parental wisdom on how to ensure that your black child survived college was honed after years of struggle, confrontation, and interaction with members of the white community. It is part of the vast repertoire of survival skills taken from the "Black Parent Survival Guide," that which is etched in our memories and orally transmitted from one generation to the next.

Ricki had been accepted to Vassar, an elite all-women's college in Poughkeepsie, New York, but she was apprehensive about the quality of black student life in upper-crust society. Instead, she chose Lorreta Heights College, in Denver, Colorado, where maternal aunts, uncles, and cousins watched over her.

The Catholic liberal arts college for women built on Ricki's strong academic foundation and intellectual curiosity. It was a perfect match. While she was one of only two black students at the college, she distinguished herself as an outgoing, gregarious young woman with enormous potential. She was a big fish in a little pond and fondly describes these years as "the black *Happy Days.*"

On weekends, she hung out with the folks in the neighborhood, where maturing into a confident, culturally conscious, young black woman was positively reinforced. The community smothered her with affection and provided a comfortable buffer to help offset the mental hazards of the all-white-girl environment.

"It was a very sweet, very supportive community. Black folks had been there for years. They had these old black southern traditions and rituals that held the community together.

"A guy would make a date with me for Friday night. He would pick me up, take me to his grandmother's house, and then to meet his mother. Afterward, we would stop by to visit with my aunts and uncles. We would go dancing on Saturday night, after we attended the NAACP meeting. Church attendance was mandatory on Sunday, and then we would sit around and play bid whist. It was, perhaps, one of the best periods in my life."

As her formal studies drew to an end, Ricki set her sights on developing her professional career. She returned home and entered graduate school at Stanford University, where she spent two years obtaining an advanced degree in journalism. Properly credentialed, her search for the good life continued.

Her first big break came in Nashville, Tennessee, where she hosted a radio program. This was followed by a stint in television, "a position that Oprah talked me into taking because she was leaving to do some television program." The irony is not lost on Ricki. Who would have thought that Oprah would end up as the nation's talk show superpower? Ricki was enjoying her local fame, until she received the long-awaited call from New York City, the one that she had been preparing for all of her life.

"I always wanted to go to New York," she explained, her voice still tinged with the excitement that she felt two decades ago. "I wanted to do news reports on black people. It was all I ever dreamed of, and my dream had come true."

Ricki spent six years in New York City as a national news anchor and United Nations reporter for the National Black Network before returning to California. Back home, she worked as a business reporter for a Silicon Valley television station. According to one local newspaper, Ricki "worked her way around the globe as a travel reporter for the San Francisco based News Travel Network." Ricki's sojourns took her to Milan, Italy, Barcelona, Spain, and Paris, France. Finally, she settled into local news as an anchor and talk show host for KRON/Bay TV in San Francisco.

During these early years, Ricki made many wise professional and business decisions that would pay off later. As she entered her thirties, her professional resume was solid. Her work experience was diverse: radio, television, and print media. The purchase of two properties—one in East Palo Alto while she was still an undergraduate student, and the other in the Silicon Valley—would bring her a financial windfall nearly thirty years later. However, attempting to make wise personal choices was a different matter.

Her first choice in a husband was a progressive, social rev-olutionary, intellectual brother who spent his days teaching at a historically black college in Tennessee. The marriage, which coincided with her break into broadcast journalism, ended before the third anniversary. After this relationship disinte-grated, she assessed her situation and decided to move on.

There were plenty of other dates, and many years in between, before she tried marriage again. Husband number two "was a brother with enormous potential but fatal flaws." Ricki was trying to follow the pathway of a blissful wonder, but it never felt right. However, the relationship lasted for five years and the union produced her one and only child.

Ricki still believed that marriage was a beautiful institu-tion. It promises love, happiness, commitment, sharing, and a bounty full of good stuff if you find the right partner. How-ever, she had given it two good shots already. She was not about to enter into a third marriage, at least not while she needed to focus the better part of her energies on raising her daughter and seeking out a life that would prove satisfying for the both of them. So she decided to wait before making another commitment to a man. She was confident in her abil-ity to provide for her daughter and raise her in a supportive, healthy environment. She was armed with professional skills and abundant ambition. Marriage to a loving partner who could also serve as an appropriate father figure for her daugh-ter might have been the preferred state, but it was not about to happen. Ricki's life started to take shape as a single-parent pro-fessional, and she was determined to make the best of it.

DARLA'S SEARCH

Darla's efforts to turn her childhood dreams into a satisfying life took her down a slightly different road. Her path was littered with social opportunities and social obstacles. After completing her high school years on the West Coast, Darla couldn't wait to return back to her roots in the East. Her choice to attend the University of Connecticut was the first step toward fulfilling her dream of becoming her own person.

"Nineteen sixty-eight had to be one of the best years to enter college," she said. "The nation was shocked by the assassination of Martin Luther King in April, and many black students felt the need to take up the gauntlet and continue the struggle. When I arrived at the University of Connecticut, all hell was about to break loose. We were able to do radical things that were a direct response to the social atmosphere that permeated the college and the nation. We planned protests, took over buildings, and made demands on the administration. I had shed my Negro looks and wore my hair in a natural. I was as black as I wanted to be. For the first time in my life, I was surrounded by a group of young black people who shared my dreams, ideals, and social customs. The camaraderie was overwhelming. It was one of the best periods in my life." And it wasn't just the academic and social environment that brought forth such pleasure. Everything was coming up rosy in the personal realm as well.

"I discovered boys. Lots of them," Darla said with obvious delight. "And I enjoyed experimenting with intimate relationships. I never thought about the risks. In my mind there weren't any. I was no longer an ugly duckling. It felt good to be a good-looking woman. My main goal was not to become pregnant, and birth-control pills took care of that."

These were heady times, indeed. And a plethora of new opportunities were created. But as Darla prepared to graduate, she still had been tracked into a traditional female field: social work. She decided to pursue a master's degree at the Jane Addams School of Social Work in Chicago. That, too, would produce memorable experiences.

"Going to Chicago was about more than getting my master's," explained Darla. "It was a period of continued maturity and a search to find out who I wanted to be. And it was about men! This was a period in my life where I took advantage of everything that was offered to me. For the first time, I understood what men wanted from women. And I knew how to work it. I enjoyed being the student. I never needed to be the aggressor. They came after me. I dated young men, older men, single men, married men, professional men, and blue-collar men. I think it is safe to say that I had a f—— good time. It took me two years to complete my master's. It probably was a good thing I was on my way out. Things started to get a little hairy. But it was a good time for me."

Darla returned to Connecticut and accepted a job as a psychiatric social worker. She talked with patients who suffered from schizophrenia, paranoia, and a variety of other forms of social neuroses. Her salary was adequate, the work environment satisfactory. But Darla didn't feel challenged by the position. One of the issues that bothered her the most was the apparent stupidity of the professionals running the system. "Who told them that they should be in charge? How did such mindless people end up in executive management?" Darla wondered. Equally disturbing was the apparent unequal treatment in the clinical services offered to blacks and whites. It appeared that whites were always viewed as the clients who had greater potential. Blacks were seen as noncompliant. Racism was definitely part of the mental health system. Dissatisfied with the professional limitations of the position, Darla quit and sought employment opportunities in a different setting.

Although she continued to have a good time, eligible black men appeared with lesser frequency. Good dates were few and far between. But Darla was not troubled. She was interested in finding true love and sharing her life with someone special, but she was not interested in getting married. This period marked the beginning of her emergence as an independent free floater. Darla would be at the center of her life. She realized that she liked having the freedom to make her own choices. Darla was living her dream, not the prescribed vision of her parents.

"I went back west to see my parents. I was about twenty-eight and had just decided to leave my job. My mother raised questions about when I was going to settle down. Translation: get married and have kids. I was pretty outraged. It brought back a flood of memories of when I was trying to be a good Negro. I didn't want anybody to tell me what to do, and I wasn't going to be forced into a role that I did not want to take. I left angry—something that I came to regret much later on."

Darla did move on, taking jobs on the supervisory level in health and human services. She was too curious to limit herself to direct service and personnel, and decided to shift her focus to health planning and administration. That's when she first started to encounter real resistance in the workforce. She had crossed over into a male-dominated field, and the men weren't too happy to see her invade their space. One instance in particular stands out in her mind.

"I was working as the administrator for the county's housing program. There was a discussion about how to best implement the governor's plan for the low- to moderate-income population. My approach and view of the situation was in sharp contrast to several of my male peers. We couldn't seem to reach an agreement. When I left the room, I overheard one guy say to another, 'How could a woman with legs like that act the way she does?' After that comment, I was always on guard. I knew what I was up against."

Darla, too, had extracted the most that she could from the social opportunities readily available in the seventies and eighties. She was a perpetual student, attending courses, seminars, and educational conferences whenever possible. She planned her career carefully. Every five or so years, she took on a new position with new challenges. She was swiftly making her way up the rough side of the bureaucratic mountain. As she entered her middle years, Darla's struggle to succeed in a male-dominated field was realized. She was the highest-paid black female in city government and just one step away from being named commissioner of a major multipurpose health organization. She owned a big house, drove a new car, and spent her free time vacationing in the Caribbean. She was a regular churchgoer with a satisfying spiritual life. A community activist, Darla was known for her efforts to improve social opportunities for inner-city youth and families. She was still childless and single and, for the moment, truly satisfied. As an independent free floater, Darla was living the life and she was absolutely certain that this was as good as it gets.

SHELLI'S SEARCH

In 1977, Shelli was on her way to the state university. Her dreams of rising to the top in the corporate world began to germinate early in her college years. College proved to be a rewarding experience. It opened up a wealth of opportunities. Shelli studied history, Spanish, and the performing arts, but finally settled on a major in business administration.

The social atmosphere was very challenging at the university. If college was a place to find a future mate, it wasn't about to happen. There were more black women than men. Too many of the black male students were athletes. Some showed little interest in black women, and only slightly more than a handful seemed committed to finishing their education as soon as possible.

Shelli was interested in a social life, even a sex life. But she wasn't willing to do the things that many other women were willing to do. She had missed the sexual revolution, but arrived just in time for the threat of herpes. The thought of multiple partners was out of the question. It was not the moral thing to do and, according to Shelli, "my mama didn't raise me like that." Besides, she had an old boyfriend from high school who she was still hanging on to. For the moment, he would have to do.

Shelli is a small, round, attractive woman. During her college years, she wore functional clothes and refused to wear makeup. She would not play the role of a fashion-conscious trophy woman. Shelli wanted to be a professional. Rather than focusing her attention on men or the lack thereof, achieving her educational goals was her top priority. Shelli was on a mission. She wanted to graduate on time, start a career in corporate America, and make her family proud.

Amid pomp and circumstance, and expressions of pride from family, extended family members, and folks in the community, Shelli graduated, on time, in the spring of 1981. She was not alone. Thousands of African American women had entered institutions of higher education and began to receive baccalaureate and graduate degrees in unprecedented numbers. Sisters were preparing to take the world by storm.

Shelli was fortunate. A large corporate utility company scooped her up before the ink had time to dry on her diploma. She was hired as a customer relations specialist. She was responsible for maintaining current accounts in the company's district one area. In accepting the position, Shelli joined a long line of black women who landed positions in the company's service-oriented, pink-collar category.

Shelli worked extremely hard. She had learned many lessons about hard work and responsibility on Aunt Sadie's farm. Thus, it was not surprising that Shelli performed exceedingly well. However, she felt that she was overqualified in her position as a customer service representative. After all, she possessed a college degree. Her co-workers did not. As other positions became available, Shelli opted to take advantage of the company's internal hiring policies. She transferred in and out of various departments, gaining great familiarity with the organization's overall operation. She had to be well versed in company operations if she expected to climb the corporate ladder. In 1985, she was finally promoted to the supervisory level, with responsibility for overseeing the work of seven employees. She had succeeded in becoming the first black woman in the company to secure a position outside of the service and pink-collar categories. She was on her way to the top.

"I was a faithful employee,'" she explained. "I worked overtime, double time, and never complained about the many assignments that were given to me. I probably was the most efficient manager that the place had ever known." At twenty-five, she was free and in control of her own destiny. She was taking full advantage of all of the benefits associated with an independent free floater.

But Shelli's life was about to take a sharp turn. One day, she ran into an old friend from the neighborhood. They accepted each other on face value and agreed that they had much in common. Their courtship lasted for a respectable period, which was of great importance to the folks in the neighborhood, and they decided to marry two years after their first date. It was a good decision. Anthony was two years older than Shelli, raised by the "same kinda folks," and shared similar values, dreams, and goals. The couple fully anticipated they would have far more satisfying lives than their parents. Theirs was not a day-to-day existence. They set educational and financial goals. They established a timetable for when they would buy property, when they would have children, and when they would retire. It seemed like the perfect union.

"I love my husband very much," Shelli says. "He is a very calm man. He takes things at a slow and steady pace. Sometimes I feel that I have to push him along to help him take the next move, but eventually he gets there." After careful consideration, Shelli had altered her path. She was now devoted to both her career and her spouse, and set about the task of balancing these two demanding roles.

Shelli's responsibilities at the utility company continued to expand. Numerous downsizing attempts led to corporate restructuring, and the number of employees under Shelli's watch increased to seventy-five. Shelli was greatly admired as the company's ideal minority employee. She served as a role model for other men and women who hoped to obtain management positions and move up in the corporate world.

"I was getting paid," bragged Shelli about her success. "The salary was good and I was happy at the job, doing what I do best. Life was sweet. But after seven years of marriage, we decided to have a baby. It was a joint decision. It would be our first and only. I had it all planned out. There was a way to do this thing—career and motherhood—and if anybody could make it work, it was me. I decided to work right up to my delivery date. After a three-month maternity leave, I would return to work and assume my responsibilities as Manager of the Year."

It was a good plan but a difficult birth. Having her first child at age thirty-four was much more difficult than she or her doctor anticipated. Complications emerged in the fourth month that required total bed rest if she expected to carry the baby to full term. Three months maternity leave extended into eight. Shelli worried about the impact that an extended leave would have on her career. Could a professional woman survive such an extended break in service? Would her new maternal status affect her ability to perform as a top-notch manager? But these were different times. Women had successfully challenged restrictive leave policies and demanded family-friendly work environments. Their skills and talents were needed in the workforce. Employers were forced to respond to a new set of social circumstances.

Ultimately, Shelli did return to her position three months after the baby was born. She picked up right where she left off as a high-level, superdedicated, energy-efficient professional. "Superstrong black woman" was a title she wore proudly.

Shelli continued to grow professionally. She considered taking additional courses at the state university and pursuing a master's degree, but she was stretched for time. She was no longer responsible for district one, but a larger area that covered the entire region. She traveled extensively around the country to partake in conferences and workshops designed to boost the efficiency of public utilities. She lived a fast-pace life, both on the road and at home. Her life was a collection of airline receipts, personal-size toiletries with hotel markings, and stacks of take-out menus stuffed in the kitchen drawer next to the avocado-colored refrigerator. She was the pride of the family. Shelli had made it to the top. She had given up her life as an independent free floater and was working hard at trying to fit comfortably into the role of a blissful wonder.

JUDITH'S SEARCH

Judith also discovered that the road to the future was brighter with higher education. And on multiple occasions, she took advantage of the educational opportunities available at predominantly white institutions.

Throughout most of her twenties, education played a prominent role in Judith's life. Judith left the shore area to take advantage of a special medical recruitment program for minority students at Widener University in Chester, Pennsylvania. She was focused on becoming a doctor—a career choice that had been assigned to her as a child by her father. The first three years of college were a breeze. Judith was bright, ambitious, and thoroughly prepared for the rigors of an academic program filled with a plethora of science courses. Biology and chemistry were her favorite subjects, and she didn't anticipate any problems with her move to the medical school. After completing the three-year accelerated program, she transferred to Hahnemann Medical College in Philadelphia.

Judith realized that she was privileged, and she felt obligated to make good on her promise to her father to pursue a medical career. Despite being tossed into an environment dominated by white males, she had to do well. Failure was not an option. Judith believed that she was just as sharp and just as bright as any other student. She wasn't seeking special treatment. She felt that she didn't need any. An offer for tutorial and support services for special admission students was summarily dismissed. She stood unflinchingly, shoulder to shoulder with her peers, and never concerned herself with the possibility of academic failure. However, she didn't anticipate having an adverse reaction to the sight of blood. It was everywhere, and she couldn't stand it. Judith quit after one year of training and decided to pursue her dreams elsewhere.

Judith considered law, computer technology, and adult education as career possibilities. Although squeamish at the sight of blood, she remained interested in the health professions. Judith turned her attention to medical transcription. She worked at Jefferson Hospital for two years. Next, she tried her hand at management. Using the people skills that she picked up as a youngster working in the family business, she accepted a position in the fast-food franchise business. In her mid-twenties and the mother a three-year-old (a pregnancy and birth she accepted without hesitation), Judith returned to school to concentrate on a degree in business administration.

Judith struggled to find her niche. Entry-level professional jobs were readily available, and her presence, sometimes as the only black worker, was nonthreatening. After all, these were not high-paying management positions, and few expected black women to aspire to loftier goals.

Before Judith turned thirty, she switched directions again, focusing on a career in public service. Working for the government provided comfort for many African Americans. The salary was good and promotional opportunities were available. More often than not, other blacks were employed in the government sector, and these jobs frequently came with civil service protection. Complaints about race and sexual discrimination could be filed with the appropriate governmental agency—for example, the Equal Employment Opportunity Commission. In fact, black folks' dependency on government and government-related jobs is disproportionate to their representation in the general population. Members of the community have often joked that if all blacks lost their government positions, it would trigger a severe economic recession in black America.

As Judith entered into a new phase of life, she had a good job, a five-year-old son, and visions of a bright future. Harry, "a loving, committed brother who accepted me and my child," was the icing on the cake. Following a brief courtship, they married and decided to settle down in the same community that had been her childhood home.

Everything seemed to fall into place. Judith had become a highly energetic blissful wonder. She garnered immense pleasure out of her multiple roles as wife, mother, and consummate professional. Having survived a difficult testing period as a single working parent, she had demonstrated to herself her ability to achieve against all odds. She had developed a passion for social change and social justice. Race and/or gender obstacles may have been a problem in the past, but she was prepared to fight for her entitlements.

CAUGHT BETWEEN TWO WORLDS

In contrast to the young women who stayed in close touch with black communities during their college years, the sisters who went to Ivy League or comparable schools found themselves battling a new enemy—alienation. Harvard, Penn, Princeton, Columbia, Brown, Dartmouth, Cornell, and Yale enjoy stellar reputations. Gaining admission to these institutions is one of the most sought-after prizes in higher education. However, only recently have these institutions accepted a barely respectable number of black students. For sisters, four years at an Ivy League school offered status, connections, and, in the view of many, the very best academic programs available in higher education. However, four years at the Ivies could also prove to be an isolating, bewildering experience.

Forty-four-year-old Patricia, a successful physician practicing in Boston, shared her experience of being accepted into Harvard. "There's something about getting that letter with the Harvard University letterhead, with a fancy crest etched in black ink at the top," she said. "You feel like you've been accepted into a different world." Florence, who attended the university in 1970, agreed. "You don't want to think of yourself as elitist. But when you realize that you're going to Harvard, your view of yourself changes. Academically, it's a wonderful place to be. The educational experience transforms your life. But it's also true what they say about blacks and Harvard . . . Harvard has ruined more brothers than a bad bottle of whiskey."

Mari, a thirty-nine-year-old Yale law graduate described her feelings about an Ivy League education as ambivalent. "You know that you're bright and you know that you belong there. But the professors and students looked at you as if you had violated their sacred ground. Some of them were very vocal about their feelings. Some of the black students were able to hang tough; others sacrificed everything to belong. We used to say, 'Yale has destroyed more minds than crack!' "

Although there was general agreement that the academics were great, "the social environment sucked." Apparently, this was especially true for black women. In a unified voice, sisters repeated the same complaint: lack of a decent social life. Scratch the surface of this complaint and the issues appeared to be one and the same: (1) Black men preferred to date white women, and (2) white men were not equally as comfortable crossing the racial divide. These factors resulted in fewer social outings and fewer dating opportunities for black women.

Cheryl, a thirty-eight-year-old writer and educator, told her story this way: "I graduated from public high school in New York in the 1980s at the top of my class. I had been a straight-A student. I got scholarship offers from so many schools it was hard to decide where to go. I selected Cornell University. I can't tell you why, except everybody was telling me it was a prestigious Ivy League school.

"My four years at Cornell were the worst in my life. I dropped from straight A's to a solid C. I don't think I had more than two dates the entire time I was there. The black male students weren't dating black women and the white boys were too afraid to ask. I graduated in four years, but I left as a bruised woman with a poor sense of self-esteem."

For one sister, preparation for the Ivy experience was set into motion long before the freshman year. The seeds were sowed in early childhood.

OLIVIA'S SEARCH

Olivia was the youngest of three daughters born to a working-class family in Boston. Her father, who was born in a small town near Macon, Georgia, left the South for the North in the early 1940s when opportunities for employment were plentiful. Olivia's mother's family had been in Boston for as long as anyone could remember and prided themselves on being proper Bostonians.

There was a sixteen-year difference between the oldest and youngest daughter. Sheila was born in 1946, just as the baby boom had gotten underway. Sheila and Olivia were half sisters—something Olivia discovered when she was in first grade. She had recently learned how to write her full name, Olivia Brown, and was eager to practice her new penmanship. She practiced her new skill by writing down each family member's name with the surname of Brown attached to it. "That's when Sheila corrected me and told me that she wasn't a Brown," Olivia said as she mimicked the diction and style of her older sister. "She was a Thomas. Thomas was her last name."

There were advantages to being the youngest of three siblings. She was doted on by every member of the family; the Browns had completed two trial runs with the older children before they turned their attention to raising Olivia. She could expect nothing but the best.

Everyone was aware of Olivia's talent. Extremely bright and fully articulate since the age of three, she was the wonder child. Olivia was pushed to do well, especially by her mother, whose dreams of higher education were cut short after she dropped out of North Carolina Central College for Negroes in 1945 when she became pregnant with Sheila. One can easily see that Olivia was a beautiful young girl. Her pixie face and large brown eyes framed by a head full of short, curly black hair still evince the sweet innocence that undoubtedly made her an adorable child.

Olivia was a model student during the first six years of public school, accelerating in every subject. But the Boston public school system was rife with tension stemming from the desegregation lawsuit. The Browns wanted to pursue another option, but as a working-class family, they had few resources to do so. Mr. Brown was a skilled factory worker and Mrs. Brown worked part-time as a nurse's aide.

Yet, unbeknownst to them, there were other forces in the community hard at work to promote racial harmony. Civic-minded nonprofit groups pushed for programs that would lead to racial integration at all levels. The ABC program (A Better Chance) was designed to improve the chances for minority children's admission to elite institutions of higher education. Founded in 1963, ABC's mission is "to substantially increase the number of well-educated minority youth capable of assuming positions of responsibility and leadership in American society." This goal is achieved by helping students from grades six through college gain access to high-quality institutions of learning. On a secondary level, this effort is achieved through placing minority students in independent private schools.

Olivia was chosen as one of the select few to participate in the program. She was plucked from her sixth-grade graduating class and awarded a full-tuition scholarship to an expensive, exclusive, all-white preparatory school for girls. For Olivia, it was the most drastic change of her life. Her experiences encompass more than twenty-five years, but the feelings of frustration and exasperation from that time are still present.

"I think that everyone expected that I would be trans-formed overnight," she said. "I went from my fashionable bell-bottom pants to school uniform—a blue blazer with a plaid, pleated skirt. I was always special in school because I was a real smart kid. Now I was special because I was a black kid. And I just wasn't any black kid, but a poor black kid from the neigh-borhood. Even though we never experienced the kind of dire poverty that was prevalent on the south side, I felt poor in comparison with all of these uppity rich white girls."

Whatever excitement was attached to being selected as a participant in this special program rapidly dissipated. The pressure to succeed was enormous. She was labeled as a spe-cial, high-achieving student at home, at church, and in the community. Added to the turbulence of adolescence was the need to prove that she was worthy of all the extra attention she was given. Her new friends and associates were different from the young sisters in the neighborhood. They affected her style, behavior, language, and diction. "Even my home girls started to ask me where I was from," she adds jokingly. "After I fin-ished the tenth grade, I decided that I just couldn't take it any-more. I had to get out of there or risk having a nervous breakdown." Against their wishes, the Browns relented to their daughter's pleas and transferred her to the public high school to complete her last two years.

It was a different world. High fashion, soul music, and ghetto slang ruled the day. Social adeptness was far more important than intellectual acuity. Olivia fell in with the right crowd and learned how to be "down." Academically, she rose prominently to her position as star. She had benefited greatly from the four years she spent at the exclusive preparatory school. Olivia graduated at the top of her class and was offered a full-tuition scholarship to an Ivy League university. It was her ticket to rejoin high society. She had been given a second chance.

Olivia's experience as an Ivy Leaguer echoed the sentiments of the other sisters. Reflecting on her four years, she now says, "As soon as you hit the campus, you know that something's not quite right. I sat in class with valedictorians from all over the country. I discovered the meaning of wealth and white privilege. I had a few dates and held on to a boyfriend all of my junior year. I spent the first part of my young adult life trying to get through an Ivy League education. I spent the last part trying to get over it. Sure I have a job, and yes, I make a good salary. But I will never do as well as my white peers. I am still a black female in America."

It seems that a privileged past can leave some of the deepest wounds to our self-esteem.

SISTER WISDOM

Young adulthood is a time of getting it together and seeing things fall apart. Even the best-laid plans are sometimes tossed asunder. Visions of a sugarplum fairy lifestyle give way to reality. Yet through it all, validating social roles slowly begin to emerge for those sisters who are resilient and looking in positive directions.

Tea's hopes of starting college after graduation from high school were delayed by her entry into the job force as a factory worker. But she quickly learned that if you want to improve your plight, you have to fight for your dreams.

Other sisters, like Terri, wander into a life of hopelessness and despair and find it's difficult to bounce back. Terri never imagined that she would be a college dropout, an officer of the law, a divorced woman, a single parent, and a drug addict all before the age of thirty. She wanted to reinvent herself, but suffered from the many poor choices that she made earlier in life. However, the Terris of the world still have time on their side. If they can get back on track in the coming decades, they will look back on their youthful experiences wondering how they ever survived.

As expectations and opportunities for black women change for the better, the best-prepared sisters rise with the tide. Olivia earned an Ivy League education. Shelli was able to obtain a degree, enter the corporate world, and finally move into a position as manager. Darla became a high-powered public official who enjoyed every bit of her life as a successful single woman living on her own terms. It was a long time coming, but after several aborted attempts, Judith and Ricki were successful in their efforts to find their own career niche.

We can find many valuable lessons born of hard-won experience during this tumultuous period.

- *Choose wisely, not foolishly.* The early choices that you make in life will have far-reaching effects on your sense of personal power. The decision to begin your young adult life at a particular institution or in a particular setting will lead you in a certain direction and will leave you with either more or less self-assuredness than you had before. The multiple consequences to your personal and professional life will continue to reverberate for years to come.

- *You don't get everything that you wish for.* Life seldom proceeds according to plan. You need to believe that despite all evidence to the contrary you can create new plans and find supportive resources when and if your life seems to take off in the wrong direction.

- *Dream big dreams.* Seize the moment and jump on opportunity. New opportunities continue to unfold for black women. Keep focused on what you want to be. Make your own decisions. You are the most qualified person to determine what you want out of life.

- *Stay on top of the vibes.* Develop an awareness of the attitudes of others that surround you. Racism and sexism are formidable obstacles. Always be on guard to protect your sense of self. Others may try to force their perceptions of "suitable" roles for black women upon you.

- *Be prepared to fight for what you want and what you believe in.* Not even privileged sisters are born with silver spoons and silver platters. Sharpen your survival skills and remain street-smart. America is not prepared for the power of black women. It is our job to make her ready.
- *Declare your independence, not your ignorance.* Strive to be your own person *and* embrace the wisdom and knowledge of your elders.
- *Stuff happens.* Your initial choices may appear devastating, but we grow from mistakes made in early life. Move on.

Black women on their way to finding satisfying lives did not think of themselves as poor, ignorant, or powerless to change their lives. There were enough windows of opportunity cracked open from time to time to keep them from desperation, if not from disappointment. Even those who seemed to have lost a connection to their former dreams believed that if they positioned themselves carefully, they could manage to take advantage of unforeseen opportunities. There would still be many challenges ahead. And for those whose lives had suddenly detoured onto thin ice, the search for the good life would continue.

4

In the Name of Love:

Surviving Early Marriage
and Motherhood

As the architects of their own future, Ricki, Darla, Shelli, Tea, Olivia, and Judith invested heavily in higher education, deciding to delay or avoid marriage and childbirth as they prepared for their careers.

Chrystal and others like her chose a different path. These young sisters offer examples of what happens when a woman discovers that planning a successful professional career might be far easier than having a successful marriage. Early childbirth and marriage continue to have the most profound impact on the lives of black women.

Motherhood permanently alters one's sense of identity. The power of motherhood is so strong that black women without children may struggle with their inability to produce them. As one sister told me:

> I grew up in a family. We all did. My parents worked hard to provide for their children. They loved us very much. I've done everything that I was supposed to do. I've completed college, got a good job, didn't get pregnant out of wedlock, and never experimented with drugs. And here I am, all by myself facing the prospect of never passing on my parents' legacy to another generation. The family line will end with me.
>
> —*Nikki, age 38*

The rewards of motherhood are enormous, but there are certainly no guarantees that everything associated with parenthood is going to work out for the best. The same can be said for the state of matrimony. In fact, marriage turns out to be one of the most rewarding and problematic challenges of the black woman's search for a satisfying role in life.

CHRYSTAL: FORCED TO MAKE A CHOICE

Chrystal's search for the Promised Land where all girls turn their dreams into reality continued to unfold in New Jersey. At twenty-three, Chrystal was a mother, a wife, and a graduate of the Gordon Marks School of Secretarial Sciences. Her daughter, Chauna, was born just eighteen months after her marriage. Chrystal and her husband purchased a starter home in Irvington, New Jersey, where they intended to stay for several years before moving on to a much larger house in East Orange.

Chrystal secured a position as an administrative assistant at the nearby university. It was a job with a title and the position paid enough to give her the sense that she had finally joined the middle class. The benefits were good, including health care, paid vacation, and tuition reimbursement to attend classes at the institution. Her husband, Richard, had accepted an entry-level business management position at Prudential Insurance Company, whose national headquarters were in downtown Newark.

Long before she turned thirty, Chrystal began to question the direction her life had taken. Why did she choose to go to secretarial school? Why did she marry a man she had known only briefly? Why did she have a baby at the age of twenty-three? In some ways, Chrystal had achieved her dreams: a caring husband, a perfect child, a lovely home, and a good-paying job. But something was not right. She was troubled by bouts of depression that occurred with greater frequency. It was difficult to locate the common ground she shared with her husband, and she found child-rearing and job responsibilities to be incompatible. As she thought seriously about her position as an administrative assistant, she came to realize that she was little more than a glorified secretary. It was time for a change.

"Since the job came with free tuition," she recalled, "I decided to go back to school and earn my bachelor's degree. I was no longer satisfied with a diploma from a trade school. I wanted to do more in life. I had to enroll part-time, and my husband was not very supportive. It meant that he had to accept more responsibility for the care of our daughter. I don't think that I ever gave it a second thought. Once I made up my mind to return to school, I wasn't going to let anything get in my way."

Chrystal spent six years at night school before graduating with honors in liberal arts. Not only had Chrystal succeeded at college, but now she was ready to pursue her master's degree in educational administration. Richard objected to the prospect of more schooling and his continued child-rearing responsibilities. More significantly, Richard felt that his wife's graduate studies would elevate her position over his own. A master's degree was out of the question. Chrystal was forced to choose between her family and career-expanding opportunities.

It has often been said that attempts at being a mother, a wife, and a professional career woman are simply too much for the average woman. "You can have two out of three," a white female senior professor told me when I was in search of my doctorate degree. But was this true for superstrong black women? Couldn't we do it all? We were raised on stories about the strength of black women, how we were always able to survive facing daunting odds—even thrive—when all others failed. Sturdy black bridges, mules of the earth, and nurturers to the world are the catchphrases that come to mind. It is part of our unique heritage. Isn't it?

AYANNA: REPAIRING A BROKEN HEART

In 1988, twenty-eight-year-old Ayanna had two children, a master's degree, and a three-bedroom skylighted home in the Mount Airy section of Philadelphia. She was employed by one of the city's largest mental health providers and, in many ways, it was the job she always wanted. Her title as psychotherapist sounded pretty prestigious when it rolled off her tongue. She was earning $32,000 a year, granted a full month's vacation, and was surrounded by human service professionals, both black and white, who she greatly admired. She enjoyed helping people and had begun to think about advanced-level training in clinical psychology. She was a blissful wonder, twice blessed. And she knew it.

Ayanna, a petite woman with shoulder-length braids and flawless skin, is surrounded by an aura of confidence. Recalling her childhood memories places her in a serene, reflective mood.

She was raised on the north side of west Philadelphia in a very poor community. Pint-sized row homes dotted the landscape up and down narrow streets with names like Race, Arch, and Vine. In search of better social opportunities during the Depression, Ayanna's paternal grandparents relocated the family from South Carolina to Philadelphia in 1933. She's unclear about the family's background on the maternal side. Her mother spoke in low, hushed tones at any mention of her grandmother. However, she does recall hearing stories about her mother and uncle being left on the doorstep of a distant relative's home in south Philadelphia.

The family background gave the appearance of being solidly working class, but Ayanna acknowledges that they were really part of the working poor. Ayanna's mother worked in a sweater factory, and her father, when he was employed, worked as a janitor. Ayanna was the oldest of six children. She knew about responsibility. She was required to watch over her younger siblings, help prepare meals, assist with the laundry, and play the roles of baby-sitter and substitute mommy. She deeply resented it. Economic pressures created additional tensions in the home. There was never enough money to pay for the basic necessities, and frivolous items such as records and stereos were simply out of the question. Ayanna's parents fought often, and sometimes her father would go away for days at a time. One day he left and never came back. Shortly thereafter, Ayanna's mother lost her job at the sweater factory and was unable to secure additional employment. She struggled, and failed frequently, to make ends meet. Public assistance was the only possible means for survival.

Ayanna spent most of her time playing outdoors. She lived in a crowded home with her five siblings and felt there was never enough privacy. Squabbles were a daily occurrence. Sometimes the focus was on violations of house rules, including borrowing each other's belongings without permission. Other infractions were minor disputes over whose turn it was to pick the television program that the family would watch. This was the era of one television per home, and TV was viewed as a luxury item. The old black-and-white 21-inch set was a permanent fixture in the corner of the living room. Ayanna loved watching cartoons, especially the *Tasmanian Devil* and *Rocky and Bullwin-*

kle, but also enjoyed watching children's programs such as *Sally Star* and *Chief Halftown* that focused on fun things for kids to do. She doesn't recall seeing black kids on these programs, but she remembers the fantasy that these shows created. As she matured, she preferred the family comedies *Bewitched* and *I Love Lucy.*

While outdoors, Ayanna perfected her skills at double Dutch and raced around the block several times each day attempting to improve her chances of being a star athlete on track-and-field day. When she was twelve, she won a blue ribbon as the best broad jumper in the city. She wanted to take home a blue ribbon each year to reinforce her sense that she was special—good at something that set her apart from her five siblings. She was an aspiring track star at Strawberry Mansion Junior High School, but she wouldn't go far. By the time she arrived at Overbrook High, she, too, wanted to participate in an activity that brought outside attention and allowed her to wear a uniform. She wanted to be a cheerleader.

"I was in the tenth grade when I decided to try out for the cheerleading squad," she explained. "I was filled with enthusiasm and loaded with energy. I had been running around the block half my life and felt that I had built up enough stamina to leap and jump and do all those other kinds of things that cheerleaders do. I didn't get picked, probably because I just wasn't good enough. But it did seem to me that light skin and long hair provided you with a better opportunity to be selected as the chosen one. That's when I started to think about the meaning of color."

Color was simply added to race as Ayanna's search for identity and a positive sense of self continued to unfold in her teen years. Based on television and her limited experience, she thought she knew the difference between black and white people. Black people lived in the city in small houses and projects; whites lived in the suburbs with big lawns. Black people were poor; white people were rich. Black parents slept together in one bed; white parents slept in two separate beds. Ayanna had more pressing issues to contend with. Did boys find her attractive? Would she have enough dates to pick and choose? Would Super Gro make her hair longer? These issues quickly dissipated when she fell in love with the man of her dreams and, at eighteen, "married him for keeps." It was a decision that would forever alter the direction of her young life, yet she still dreamed of being somebody. When her first child was born, just six months later, her vision of the future was quite clear. She would take courses at the community college, continue to work part-time as a salesgirl, have three more children before she turned thirty, and find a lovely little home in Mount Airy.

In the late 1970s when Ayanna graduated from high school there were many new opportunities available to black women. Early marriage was not the only way to escape from home, flee from poverty, or hide an unexpected pregnancy. In fact, those choices were becoming less popular options with each new graduating class. By the early 1980s, the pressure to marry and have children before the age of twenty-five had lessened considerably. The advent and wide-scale use of birth-control pills in the 1960s gave women the option to prevent unwanted pregnancies. And, if an accidental pregnancy occurred, unrestricted abortions were available.

Educational opportunities were plentiful, particularly access to courses on the community college level. Businesses, corporations, and governmental agencies employed black women to provide a multitude of professional and support services. Moreover, black female participation in professional occupations increased. They were teachers, preachers, politicians, doctors, lawyers, and scientists. Opportunities were available if sisters desired to pursue these avenues, although they were still somewhat limited. Ayanna believed that she could juggle the responsibility of being a wife, mother, and college student. And she succeeded. Ayanna completed her undergraduate studies before her youngest child turned three.

Now she was contemplating another degree. If Ayanna wanted to pursue a doctorate degree in psychology or any other field, Philadelphia was the right place to be. Although rarely cited for its reputation as a college town, the region is home to more than thirty institutions of higher education. After mulling over her available choices, with special consideration given to financial issues, Ayanna chose Temple University.

"I had big plans. First, I was going to enter Temple University and complete my studies in three years. I was going to keep my full-time job, although they did give me time off to pursue my course work. Following graduation, I would open up my own practice and work exclusively with black families. I was a member of the Association of Black Psychologists and had been exposed to the writings of people like Bobby Wright, Na'im Akbar, and Wade Nobles. I thought they were on to something. I wanted to practice from a black perspective."

Ayanna was secure at home, adored her two children who she described as "my greatest inspiration," and was in the process of implementing her professional plans. It was often suggested to her that she was doing too much, but she never heeded the warnings. She was a highly energetic young woman who squeezed all that she could out of life. But her well-laid plans were about to be shattered.

"I was sitting at my desk when the call came in. It was shortly after a counseling session with a lesbian couple. I had never counseled two women before and I struggled with my feelings of homophobia. I wasn't certain that I was doing or saying the right thing and I wanted to be as professional as possible. When the phone rang, I anxiously picked it up, thinking it was my supervisor. I knew he wanted to see me about that last session. Instead of my supervisor's voice, it was my husband's.

" 'Go get checked,' is all that he said. 'Go to the doctor and get yourself checked.' That was the best he could do in telling me that I had been exposed to a sexually transmitted disease."

Ayanna doesn't recall whether she was treated for syphilis or gonorrhea. She remembers balling her eyes out in the doctor's office and being given a regimen of pills along with a shot of penicillin in her butt. The older white male doctor tried to comfort her, advising her that if she still loved her husband, she needed to forgive him and move on.

The marriage deteriorated rapidly. Ayanna and her husband went through a trial separation followed by a brief reconciliation. But there was no longer enough trust in the relationship for it to continue.

" 'Stand By Your Man' is the song that comes to mind. I just wasn't going to do it. Not me. I refused to accept the role as the dutiful, forgiving wife. I realized that the affairs were part of our relationship and it was clear to me that my husband wanted to move on. I finally let him go. It was the hardest thing that I ever had to do. I didn't want to be by myself. In fact, I was afraid of being alone, but I was not going to hold on to a messy marriage. I had two small children and knew that $32,000 was not going to take me very far. And I suspected that once my husband walked out of the door, he would disappear from our lives forever. I never gave any thought to abandoning my role as a mother. That was the one thing I was certain I would continue to do."

Ayanna's life on her pathway as a blissful wonder ended. She could have turned her head away from her husband's infidelities and remained in her marriage, but she chose not to do so. And she recognized that the ramifications of her decision would be far-reaching. At the age of twenty-eight, Ayanna was faced with a brand-new challenge. Could she achieve a happy and satisfying life as single-parent professional?

ROSLYN: SEEKING AN ESCAPE

Roslyn's marriage started out with a bang. It was just the beginning of an emotionally charged, roller-coaster lifestyle that would have proved challenging to any teenager. Her father and stepmother had barely recovered from the shock of their daughter's marriage on the night of her high school graduation when Roslyn called and informed them that she was on her way overseas. Today, Roslyn is a wife and mother of three. A tall, thickly built woman with a fair complexion, she keeps her shoulder-length dark brown wavy hair presentable by brushing it back to the nape of her neck and securing it with a rubber band.

Born in 1961 in St. Louis, Missouri, she was the eldest of two children born to Johnny and Anna Slate. A mere ten months separated the two births. The family moved frequently from the city to small surrounding towns as they took turns staying with different relatives. Both parents possessed a high school diploma, but good jobs were hard to come by.

Roslyn enjoyed playing a lot of hand games with her younger sibling and with the kids on the block. Clapping, singing, and twirling all around were required. She begins to sing:

Miss Mary Mack, Mack, Mack,
All dressed in black, black, black,
With silver buttons, buttons, buttons,
All down her back, back, back.

She remembers running home after school to see *Dark Shadows* and her favorite cartoon show, *Speed Racer*, which, she recalls, was the first television show she was able to view in color. Again she sings:

Here he comes, here comes Speed Racer
He's a demon on wheels . . .
He's a demon and he's gonna be chasing after someone.

In 1966, Roslyn entered elementary school in the midst of the civil rights struggle. "It was a segregated school in a racially segregated neighborhood," she recalled. "In fact, everything about those early years was black. I really don't remember having many interactions with white folks until I was bused to a racially mixed school in the third grade. I didn't know what to make of it. It wasn't like I hadn't been exposed to white people before. There were white people in my family. No one ever said so, but I'm pretty sure that my father's mother was white. Well, in her own mind she was a Native American. She never claimed to be black. I always knew that there were white people in the world; they just didn't live in my community."

When Roslyn entered elementary school, *Brown v. Board of Education*, the landmark 1954 Supreme Court decision to end school desegregation, was more than a decade old. Yet the pace of integration was slow. At the same time, expectations for change were high as thousands took to the streets to protest racial discrimination in America. Social expectations for change lagged far behind social reality. Blacks continued to live on the periphery of society.

Roslyn's world was shattered when her mother died suddenly from a disease called lupus. No one had ever heard of the disease before it struck a member of the family. Lupus is a debilitating autoimmune disease that attacks healthy cells and causes inflammation and damage to tissues, joints, and organs. Its sufferers are disproportionately female (nine out of ten), with black women accounting for roughly 25 percent of those diagnosed. Little was known about the causes and treatment of lupus thirty years ago when it claimed Roslyn's mother's life.

It was an unbearable loss for Roslyn's father. He gathered his two children and went searching for a new life and a better place to live in the Northeast. He landed in a semirural community in Pennsylvania where a small group of black families resided in the midst of a white farming community.

The downtown area was a two-block strip with all the necessary suppliers: a pharmacy, hardware store, corner grocery, butcher shop, and coffeehouse. The strip was anchored at one end with the only gasoline station in town; on the opposite end was the town's municipal buildings, including the post office, library, and one-man police department.

Life was simple. All the black people lived within walking distance of each other's homes in a racially segregated part of town. And all the blacks who attended church worshiped at First Zion Baptist. However, other forms of segregation were more difficult to maintain. All the children attended the same elementary school and were later bused to junior and senior high schools that serviced the entire region. There were spring, summer, fall, and winter festivals that brought out members of the entire community. Roslyn fondly recalls this period as a time when "all the people tried to get along. It was a really good experience."

Within a few short years of his move, Mr. Slate remarried, and two additional children were added to the family. It was sometimes lonely being the only girl, and Roslyn felt the relationship with her father had been strained by the addition of his new wife. In addition, Roslyn's father had developed a serious drinking problem. When in a drunken stupor, he was mean, vicious, and venomous to every member of the family.

For a brief period, Roslyn was sent back to Missouri to live with her maternal grandmother, but returned just in time to enter high school in the tenth grade with the graduating class of 1979.

Roslyn certainly was bright and encouraged to do well by her teachers, but she wasn't really interested in education. Her focus was on gaining her independence and placing herself in a situation where she could do just about anything that she wanted. She frequently fought with her parents, had minor squabbles with her three brothers, and began to feel that she was located in a hick town that wasn't even on the map.

As a graduation present to her parents, Roslyn arranged to meet her father and stepmother at the church, where she surprised them by marrying her twenty-year-old boyfriend of ten months just hours after she received her diploma. She packed her belongings in a blue suitcase as she prepared to leave home. The radio was playing the Carpenters' tune "We've Only Just Begun."

Lacking advanced training and marketable job skills, Roslyn's young husband soon discovered that military service would be his best option. Following the completion of basic training at Fort Bragg in North Carolina, he was given an overseas assignment in Germany. Something stirred in Roslyn at that point. Her world suddenly expanded. She viewed the assignment as an opportunity to take a whirlwind vacation.

"I think the best thing about the marriage was that I had the opportunity to travel. I don't think that I would have visited Europe if my husband were not in the army. Of course, it's never like you think it's going to be. After the excitement wore off, I became a little homesick. There were a lot of things I didn't like about the army, especially the medical service. When I became pregnant, I knew that I did not want my child born in an army hospital.

"If your husband is in the military and you live in an area where army hospitals are not available, you get to go to the hospital of your choice. The military will pay for it. I returned back to the States before my son was born. I was looking to stay with a family relative who didn't live near a military hospital. I ended up in Florida." Roslyn's son was born just fifteen months after her marriage.

When her husband returned from his tour of duty, they settled down near the base. While she was consumed with child-rearing responsibilities, he was involved in criminal activity. After several unsolved burglaries on the military base, he was identified as the culprit, court-martialed, and incarcerated for six months. Later, he was dishonorably discharged.

"I did not think that this was part of marriage," Roslyn said. "In addition to his legal troubles, I discovered that he was seeing another woman on the base. I wanted to end the marriage, but I kept reminding myself of my vow, 'until death do us part.' I decided to stick it out.

"Because of the difficulty we were having, I went back home to my parents. When my husband was released [from prison], he came and got the baby and me and moved us to New York.

"We were only there for a few months when I saw the woman from the base and realized that my husband had brought her along, too. I said to myself, 'God did not intend for you to suffer.' It [the marriage] was over after that. I had to gather up my strength to walk away. I would be returning back home and everyone would know that I had made a mistake, just like my stepmother said."

NASHEA: PLAYING THE ROLE

Nashea always believed that her life would be fabulous. Some of her fondest memories as a young child were of the days she spent swinging on a wooden swing that her father built just outside the home he had constructed from scratch. Nashea's family was from a long line of homeowners. Her great-grandfather purchased land in Delaware and built his own home in the early 1900s. His sons and grandsons followed in his footsteps.

Most of the family lived within walking distance of each other in the segregated community. Aunts, uncles, cousins, and a host of other relatives surrounded Nashea. It was a close-knit extended family community whose members exerted a great amount of influence and control over Nashea's life. They, too, lived like country folks. There was a garden to grow food. In the summers, the garden produced sweet corn, tomatoes, green beans, squash, and cucumbers. The collard greens would continue to grow right up to Thanksgiving. The public streets, where Nashea often had to navigate her red and blue bicycle, were a mix of clay, gravel, and black dirt. Asphalt roads existed in another part of town. Outside influences, especially television viewing, were kept to a minimum. A high level of racial segregation existed in Delaware and throughout the region. Nashea, too, lived in a black world.

Even as a young child, Nashea knew she was going somewhere. She was certain that she would be somebody. As she watched the frequent airplanes fly overhead, she dreamed of one day taking her seat on a jumbo jet and flying off to faraway places. The destination wasn't important. Getting away from the family was. Nashea was not going to follow in her mother's footsteps: too many children, too much heartache, and a life completely dominated by her husband. She tells of the tremendous impact that her father had on her life.

"My dad was a rigid man. With the precision of a military drill sergeant, he dictated the daily schedule for the entire family. Everyone would rise at 6 A.M. Breakfast was served at seven, lunch at noon, and dinner at half past five. It never changed." Nashea's father was an assembly-line worker at a nearby factory that produced automotive parts. He worked twenty-two years before calling in for a sick day. A devout Christian man, his life was devoted to his job and family.

Nashea was anxious to leave home as soon as possible. Her adventurous spirit, coupled with a heavy surge in adolescent hormonal activity, produced friction in the household.

During her high school years, she was sent to live with relatives across town to help temper her rebellious nature. Getting to and from the regional high school was a major challenge, but she survived. She found her own clique of best friends who enjoyed dancing, gossiping, and hanging out at the local sandwich shop. By sixteen, Nashea started to plan her getaway.

"From the very beginning, I knew that I was not going to work in a setting that restricted opportunities for black women," she proclaimed on the afternoon we sat in her comfortable home for the interview. "And I also knew that I would move through life at my own pace. I graduated from high school early, took a packed course load at the university, and was off to Europe in no time." While the events that shaped her life started to unfold more than thirty years ago, Nashea relays the story with a great deal of pride. She was barely twenty-one when she stepped off the plane in Europe in the summer of 1973 and became an instant celebrity. It was a completely unique experience. Celebrity status came easily, and Nashea had no difficulty fulfilling the role.

"When African Americans arrived in Europe at the peak of the civil rights and black power movement, people viewed them as exotic," she said. "I was a curiosity, especially in Italy, where everyone seemed so interested in life back in the States. When you were introduced as an African American, it was as if you were a foreigner with a special status. It was different from being introduced as a person from the African continent." Eventually, she fell in love with a gorgeous Italian man and embraced his family, community, and culture as her own.

"Once I got married, I had guaranteed access to influential social circles. I traveled with the wealthy upper-class folks. It was nothing for me to get dressed in the finest clothes, have lunch at the best restaurants, and then take in a fashion show of the major designers of the day. Sophia Loren might be seated to my right, some other famous person to my left. It was nothing for me to be seated right there in the front row." And she enjoyed every minute of it.

However, there were other activities in Nashea's life. Her marriage and the birth of her son occurred in rapid succession. She needed to fulfill family obligations. In addition to caring for her son with the help of a nanny and a housekeeper, she remained responsive to the needs of her husband. And while she enjoyed playing the role of a rich man's wife, she was a sister.

Nashea used her expertise in economics and finance to make forays into the social fabric of community life. She worked with television, radio, and other media outlets seeking an American perspective on contemporary issues. She consulted with business and city officials on presentations targeted to American businesspeople and hosted some events for local entrepreneurs. Nashea became involved in charitable causes and organized special events for the underprivileged. Her life had taken shape as a blissful wonder and these were among the happiest days of her life. With all the support that she ever needed, Nashea achieved a near-perfect balance between her personal and professional needs. During her free time, she continued to work at perfecting her skills as a diva. She invested fifteen years in the project before the job was completed.

Kalilah: The Writing on the Wall

No one's story better epitomizes the riskiness of a relentless search for a fulfilling intimate life than Kalilah's. An attractive, fair-skinned woman with lashes the length of Bambi's, Kalilah was born in Los Angeles, California. She was the third of three children. Her father was a self-taught auto mechanic who spent all of his time tinkering with cars. Her mother was a housewife. Kalilah recalls that her mother always tiptoed around her father's needs. After a hard day's work, nothing was to upset him. He had a volatile temper and the slightest incident could cause an explosion.

Kalilah's father, a hardworking man, was always looking for work, yet he was a good provider who secured the family a ranch-style home and other necessities. Kalilah's mother often told her stories about how Kalilah's father struggled to make ends meet before and after the Second World War. Employment opportunities, which were plentiful during the war economy, began to dry up after victory was secured. Kalilah's father traveled afar seeking employment, often passing himself off as a white man in order to take positions that discriminated against people of color. "My father was white-looking with dark hair," she recalled. "But I never had any doubt that I was black. My mother was a brown-skinned woman and we took some of our color from her. I also remember my mother telling me how my father made a conscious decision to marry a woman who was dark enough to make sure that no one would ever mistake his children for anything other than black. He had a very difficult time as a child in the black and white community. He grew up in a very poor section in New Orleans, Louisiana. People would tease him, beat him up, and call him names like 'white bastard' and 'white nigger.' I think some of that is what made him so mean." Kalilah's earliest childhood memories are focused around the need to keep a secret, especially from her father.

"When I was about five years old," she recalls vividly, "I was accidentally scalded down the front of my chest by a foster child that was staying with us. She picked up a boiling pot from the stove and was unable to hold on to it. When the pot hit the floor, I got caught in the crossfire. My mother was fearful of my father's reaction, so she told me not to tell my father." It was a shared secret between mother and daughter. No one else was to know.

Kalilah lived in a racially mixed neighborhood. Sometime during the second grade, she became aware of her blackness and the negative connotation associated with race and skin color.

"It was a minor incident. I can't even recall all the details. The white kids yelled at me and called me colored. Just the way they said it struck a cord of negativity in my soul. I knew it wasn't pleasant. And I knew that my father would be upset if he knew that something bad happened to me. It was another secret I kept to myself."

Kalilah's next big secret occurred while she was still in the second grade.

"I think I was seven or eight. I don't know what season it was, but I was outside playing with my coat on. My brother, who is six years older than me, was entertaining his friend in the garage area near the house. It [the garage] wasn't attached to the house like they are now. My older sister was in our bed-room and she could see what was going on from the window.

"I adored my brother and always wanted to be anywhere that he was. When I went to the garage, he was not there, but his friend Jimmy was. He was thirteen. He put me up on the table and lifted up my dress. He told me to pull down my panties and he would show me something. He opened his pants and pulled out his penis. I'm certain that I'd never seen one before. He made me touch it. It was traumatizing. I was sitting there, waiting to be penetrated, when my sister, who was four years older than me, and my mother, burst in the door. My sister could see what was happening from the bed-room window. She ran into the kitchen and got my mother. They reached me just in time.

"I knew I had done something wrong. My mother scolded me and told me never to tell my father, never tell my brother, and never tell anyone what had happened. I kept the secret to myself until I turned forty."

When Kalilah was eight years old, her father suffered a fatal heart attack. His death left the family struggling to make ends meet. The economic pressure was overwhelming, as every mem-ber of the family struggled to make a financial contribution.

As soon as they reached their eighteenth birthday, both Kalilah's brother and sister left home to strike out on their own. Kalilah was left with her mother, who became overly dependent, emotionally and financially, on her daughter.

As she matured, Kalilah encountered some of the difficul-ties experienced by adolescent girls: petty jealousies, social insecurities, physical transformations, and, in general, worries about her ability to do well in life. Her failure to pass the ninth-grade entrance exam for the Catholic high school was the first real indicator that she was unable to compete with her peers. Forced to attend the public high school, she wanted to make a new start and find acceptance among her new friends.

Kalilah met Billy when she was seventeen years old and a junior in high school. Anxious to please and wanting to project an image of confidence and sophistication, she agreed that engaging in sexual intercourse was the mature thing to do. Much to her surprise, she became pregnant shortly thereafter. If birth-control methods were generally available, no one had told her anything about it. She was never privy to discussions about sexual intercourse, childbirth, or pregnancy prevention. In the late 1960s, pregnancy out of wedlock was still treated with a great deal of disdain. Kalilah's mother insisted that the two young lovers be married.

"My mother decided to have this shotgun wedding. My brother was opposed to me getting married because he, too, had been forced to marry a girl that he got pregnant. I wanted to get married to get away from my mother. She arranged for us to stay with her until we could get on our feet and find a place of our own. After the wedding, I packed my bags and went home with my new husband, to his mother's house. That is when I knew that it wasn't going to work. It lasted for about four months until I was forced to return back home."

A baby girl was born in the spring. Kalilah was eighteen, unemployed, and dependent on welfare. Seeing no purpose in continuing a marriage that was doomed from the start, she divorced her husband and started anew.

Lenny was smart, good-looking, and twenty-one. The relationship was good; the sex was hot. Kalilah discovered that she was pregnant, again, less than six months after the birth of her first child. She wanted to establish herself as an independent, responsible black woman. She wanted to do the right thing. She was convinced that she should give marriage a second try. Kalilah married Lenny in a much smaller, civil ceremony. She had a new set of in-laws who were accepting of her and her first-born, and anxiously awaiting the birth of Lenny's child.

The baby was adorable. Although they had two different fathers, the siblings looked very much alike. Unfortunately, the relationship with Lenny became strained. Too much pressure, too little money, and too little privacy were part of the problem. Six months later, the relationship was over and Kalilah returned home to her mother and filed for a divorce.

Barely twenty, Kalilah sought a different approach. She pulled up stakes and moved farther north to Oakland. This was an effort to sever her close dependent ties with her mother who always had a great influence over Kalilah's life. She had gained her independence but was unemployed. Welfare was her only option.

Kalilah's search for a meaningful life continued. As a member of the Black Panther Party, she engaged in social activism, protesting social injustices and spewing revolutionary slogans at anyone within earshot. She joined the Nation of Islam, changing her name and accepting an X. Later, she wrapped herself in cultural garb and searched for her cultural center. She experimented with alcohol and drugs including marijuana, acid, speed, and cocaine. At twenty-two, Kalilah became pregnant for the third time. The baby's father proposed marriage, but Kalilah wanted the opportunity to experience a marriage that was not clouded by an impending birth. Desperately wanting to avoid another failure, she terminated the pregnancy and the relationship, and decided to move on.

When Kalilah met Max, she had two small children and an empty womb. She was far more worldly and hoped that this relationship would signal the beginning of a stable family life. She was confident in her ability to make a fresh start. No longer on the welfare rolls, she now worked two jobs to help make ends meet. She decided to give marriage another try.

"My first two marriages suffered from the strain of being pregnant," she insisted. "This was not going to be a problem in my third marriage. Ironically, just as I had begun to see that I could make it on my own, my level of confidence seemed to threaten my new husband. The marriage lasted for about two years before it was over."

By her twenty-fifth birthday, Kalilah had been married and divorced three times. She had been pregnant four times, two ending in live births and the other two ending in abortions—one legal and the other illegal. She had two children in grade school. She was employed most of the time, but consistently rotated on and off welfare until she could get herself together. She had gained considerable weight. She left the movement, left the Mosque, ended her quest to be African, but continued to do drugs and hang out in bars. Her search for the good life continued. Finally, she thought she found true happiness when she met Harry, who was destined to be husband number four.

Harry didn't appear to be much different from husbands number one, two and three. He was a working-class brother with limited marketable job skills. He worked from nine to five. He was an apprentice in a print shop, struggling to learn the trade from the master. Kalilah was a good-looking, fair-skinned, full-figured woman with long, flowing hair. She never suffered from lack of male attention. "I never had any trouble attracting men," she states. "That's something that was not a problem for me." However, finding the key to happiness proved elusive. Kalilah admits that she was confused about the nature of male–female relationships. Her father died when she was a young child, and what she remembers of the relationship between her father and mother was "something strange." Yet, she continued to use her relationships with men as a way of finding her identity. She was convinced that marriage number four would be different. And she was right. For the first time in her life, Kalilah was introduced to domestic violence.

None of our Cinderella dreams include visions of relationships marred by verbal, physical, and emotional abuse. Domestic violence, once silently condoned as private affairs that took place within the sacred realm of the household, emerged as a major social issue in the 1970s. Women no longer wanted to be silenced by abusive partners and ignored by law enforcement officers and court officials who trivialized their accounts of abusive attacks by loved ones.

Sisters may suffer the pain of domestic violence more acutely. Stereotypical images of the "grits throwing," "lye-burning," "kick-your-butt," "bad-ass superstrong black woman" did not resonate with the sisters in this investigation. Those who experienced domestic violence described their experiences as terrifying. Physical abuse brought black eyes, busted lips, broken bones, and threats against life. But the emotional and sexual abuse proved to be just as devastating.

Jasmine is a forty-three-year-old education professional. She earned a four-year degree from a predominantly white, state-supported institution in Michigan. Jasmine believes that she is physically attractive, "in an African sort of way." She can wax poetic on any subject from politics to foreign affairs. Jasmine is single, childless, and suspects that she will remain that way for the rest of her life. She turned her life over to Jesus in her early twenties and established herself as a faithful follower. She was a devout believer, proselytizing to those who did not know the blood of Christ. She was secure and in control of her life. As she entered her middle phase, her life took off in an unfamiliar direction.

"I had lots of free time on my hands, so I decided to do some volunteer work," said Jasmine. "I've always been interested in challenging situations. When I was asked to serve as a tutor for the state prison, I took a leap of faith and decided to share my knowledge and expertise with those who were less fortunate.

"It's true what they say about prisons. Brothers were everywhere. Men who wouldn't speak to you on the street were bending over backward to offer you compliments. Against my better judgment, I became involved with one of the prisoners. After the honeymoon period, he became very controlling and emotionally and verbally abusive. I couldn't believe that a man who was incarcerated could take such control over my life. I was not a young, dumb, and foolish woman . . . maybe a middle-aged desperate one. I stayed in the relationship for two years. I lost all of my self-esteem and had to seek therapy to overcome the emotional consequences. And I lost my faith in the process—which was a long time coming. I guess church folks would describe me as a backslider."

Jasmine never endured physical assault. Her lover of two years was, after all, incarcerated in the state prison. Kalilah wasn't as fortunate. Her fourth husband was verbally, sexually, and physically abusive. He seemed to be in a constant state of rage. "It was unbelievably bad. I thought, *this could not be happening in my life.* I felt trapped and fearful of leaving. I found myself constantly thinking about an escape plan. Finally, I called my cousins and made arrangements to take my belongings and leave the house while he was away at his job. I left most of my material possessions. All I wanted was to get the kids, get away, and be safe."

As Kalilah approached thirty, her only true accomplishment was her ability to raise her two children alone and keep them out of foster care. And that, in and of itself, was a monumental task. She found steady employment in the school district and she started to understand the meaning of life. Her children were approaching their teens and she worried about the amount of nurturing they received. Realizing that the next several years would be critical to their growth and development, she finally gave up drugs and nightly visitations to local bars. Her children provided the strength she needed to alter her life. She was working steadily, but was unable to establish herself in a comfortable lifestyle. Again, she took on a second job to help boost her income.

Kalilah was not a single-parent professional; rather, she was a single working parent who constantly struggled with limited resources to provide for her offspring. Malik, a sweet-looking, smooth-talking, deep chocolate brother with a medium-sized Afro, offered her another ray of hope.

Malik was everything that Kalilah had hoped for. God had sent her a dreamboat, and she hadn't even prayed for him. He was employed as an engineer. He owned property in the southeast section of the city. He was a man of comfortable financial means. Malik showered her with gifts, responded affectionately to her two children, and shared his dreams about their future together as a family. Kalilah was swept off her feet. She was hesitant to enter into another marriage, but decided to roll the dice one more time. Malik was a precious find, and she couldn't let him get away. They married on Valentine's Day in a romantic evening ceremony. Malik moved his belongings into her home and settled in to enjoy a blissful, comfortable life.

It wasn't long before Kalilah discovered that husband number five was a lying, cheating man. She had been won over with a facade of deception. Malik didn't have a job, didn't own property, and, with the exception of the belongings that he arrived with when he moved into her home, had no assets of any kind. What Malik needed was a woman who was willing to provide for him, and Kalilah fell right into his trap.

Embarrassed about her own naivete and vulnerability, Kalilah tried to make the marriage work. She encouraged her husband to seek employment, talked about new beginnings, and attempted to motivate him to take a new direction in life, all to no avail. After a year of struggling, her decision to seek a divorce was a no-brainer. But she was troubled by her repeated failure to establish a lasting relationship. Did she make poor choices? Did she lack the commitment and wherewithal to make a difficult marriage work? Was she the victim or the perpetrator?

At the age of thirty-two, Kalilah decided to give up her search for the perfect spouse. In a fourteen-year period, she endured five brief marriages. No one else could match her matrimonial record. Her efforts to secure a partner had failed over and over. She had not found happiness. She questioned the meaning of marriage and her understanding of the institution. Did she ever really know what a relationship should be between a man and a woman? How it should function? What are the elements of give and take? Kalilah was no longer as strikingly attractive as she was when she was a much younger woman. And having good looks no longer mattered. She thought the search had ended for good. Economic survival and the ability to raise her two children would be her only focus. What else did life have to offer?

Sister Wisdom

For these young sisters, marriage and children were the first major choices that shaped the direction of their lives. The marriage, if untenable, could be terminated; but the role of mother would last forever. While the children were viewed as a blessing, the advice for the next generation remains timeless and crystal-clear: *Wait until you are secure and mature enough to understand your own wants and needs before you bring children into the world.*

Succeeding at school, getting a satisfying job, being rewarded with a promotion, and making your mark as a contributing member of society are other factors that sisters use to measure their success during young adulthood. But this is only part of the equation. Seeking a balance between your personal life and professional life is a desired goal, but a difficult and time-consuming one. The pathway to personal happiness may be perilous and unpredictable. The sisters discussed in this chapter encountered it all in search of a few good men. For these young sisters, the search for the good life usually included turmoil.

Black women were both beneficiaries and victims of the sexual revolution. Free sex, birth control, abortion, and no-fault divorces all became readily available in the years that black women emerged as leaders in single-parent households. Sisters were frequently thwarted by poor choices in partners. Yet they were able to detach themselves from destructive marriages and make plans to start anew.

What important lessons were gleaned from this period that bear reinforcing today?

- *Cherish your children.* Offer unconditional love to your offspring. It keeps you focused, motivates you to achieve your goals, and puts you closer to the good life.

- *Love doesn't always last forever.* What is often mistaken for everlasting love may only be lust, desire, or confusion. Immaturity and lack of knowledge about adult roles and responsibilities may cause you to tumble in your young adult years.
- *If at first you don't succeed at love and marriage, don't stress.* Cut your losses and get on with your life. This is only your first marriage.
- *Read the writing on the wall.* Things don't just happen. There are warning signs. Rely on your intuition. Listen to your inner voice. Take threats to your life seriously. Free yourself from intolerable situations while you still have the strength to do so.
- *Watch how he treats his mother.* His attention to your needs will be about the same.
- *Be a self-determining sister.* Self-discovery and self-determination are driving forces as you mature and move toward midlife. Make it a priority to define your own needs and discover how you want to shape your identity. Don't live vicariously through others. Claim your space and do your own self-defined thing.
- *Take chances, even if no one you know has done so before.* Most of life's achievements can be credited to the willingness and ability to pursue your goals. A certain amount of risk taking is necessary. Be cautious, not foolish. But be willing to venture into new territory.

- *Don't wait for your ship to come in or expect your man to be your captain.* All men are not created captains. Rather than sink or wait around, get your own boat, take the helm, and sail off to your chosen destination.

As the sisters in this chapter began midlife, they struggled to redefine themselves as positive, mature black women. How could they capture the essence of their youthful identities? They shared a heightened awareness that crunch time was here. Their innocence had been washed away by their experiences, but the next phase in life promised more new beginnings. They still viewed themselves as women with plenty of time ahead.

5

The Black Woman's Burden:

Disruptions and Stress

A re we ever permitted to disconnect ourselves from the past? Can we continue to move forward, sometimes leaving family and friends behind, as we chase our dreams for a brighter future? Is it ever the morally defensible thing to do? These questions emerge again and again as we continue our pursuit of a satisfying life.

The ability of so many black women to achieve against all odds is truly remarkable when viewed in the context of the black experience in America. Many advances in the black community in the last half of the twentieth century merit celebration. We are reminded of the old adage, "We're not where we wanna be, but thank God we're not where we used to be." But even the most promising efforts that we make to lift ourselves up by our bootstraps and elevate the status of our families and communities can be sabotaged by developments beyond our control.

ROSLYN'S CHALLENGE

Once Roslyn discovered that her husband of two years had been having an affair with his old flame from the military base, Roslyn ended her first marriage and took on the role of a single parent. She was only twenty. Unskilled and lacking any form of advanced education, she stoically hopped from job to job, seeking the highest salary that an employer would offer. Roslyn was from a poor working-class family. When her mother died, a small policy was available to cover burial expenses. And that was all. The concept of inheritance was not part of her world. Her family could offer her love and guidance, but no financial support.

As a struggling young mother, Roslyn cleaned offices before moving on to a job as a telemarketer. She was in a constant struggle to make it on her own. Her performance as a breadwinner was barely adequate, and she recognized that she was, indeed, poor. However, welfare was not an option. Roslyn was from a proud family whose members would do whatever necessary to survive. Taking government handouts was never encouraged. Facing the double-barrel threat of poverty and homelessness, Roslyn returned home to live with her father and stepmother.

Just after her twenty-fifth birthday, Roslyn met Robert, a hardworking professional who was looking for a serious relationship. A proposal for marriage soon followed. Robert brought the promise of love, happiness, and economic stability. Roslyn and Robert settled down near Hartford, Connecticut, and added a few more children to the family.

Roslyn enjoyed every bit of the good life. She lived in a large, beautiful home in a safe, predominantly white community. Her children attended high-quality educational institutions, and she was readily available to support them in all of their extracurricular activities. Her husband adored her. Extended family members were within driving distance of the family home, and there was never any question about the amount of love and affection that was spread throughout. She was happy beyond belief.

Roslyn was well into her thirties when she first tried part-time work. It was a low-wage job close to home with a flexible schedule. She was able to drop the children off early in the morning and pick them up early in the afternoon. But the responsibility of work and home was too burdensome. It placed additional stress on her life and the family. She relinquished her job and returned home to focus on her domestic responsibilities.

A few years later, Roslyn decided to return to school to pursue an associate's degree. She was interested in teaching in the public school system and was fully aware of the need for a college degree. However, this, too, caused additional strain, and Roslyn decided to delay her educational plans until after her youngest child graduated from high school. She would be about fifty, still young enough to think about establishing a career.

Roslyn realized that she was perfectly happy being a domestic warrior. It was a time-consuming, demanding job that she loved, and she was willing to make personal sacrifices to ensure that her family remained her top priority. She was not going to be forced into a role that she didn't want. Roslyn had a husband in a high-pressure job. He was a black man in a white corporate environment. He needed someone to care for him when he returned home from a difficult day's work. Her three children also needed special attention. The youngest was an eight-year-old son whose hyperactivity required her to stay on top of the school's attempts to classify him as a special needs child. The middle child was a talented twelve-year-old performing artist, and the oldest was her eighteen-year-old son, Lance. He was the product of the first marriage and, much to her dismay, completely strung out on drugs.

Lance's drug problems came as a stunning surprise to everyone in the family. "I don't know that we were fully aware of what was going on until it happened," Roslyn said. She is pensive as she poignantly reveals the pain and heartache that accompany every parent's nightmarish story about the destructive consequences of drug abuse and addiction.

"Lance wasn't doing well in school. He never was an exceptionally good student, but it was pretty clear that he was going to fail high school. He started to fabricate stories about his life. We couldn't get a clear picture of what was really going on. For the first time in his life, he got into trouble with the law. Breaking and entering. . . . We spent a lot of money trying to keep him out of jail. Everybody has tried to talk to him about his future. I think he's depressed, but no one ever diagnosed him in that way." Roslyn laughed nervously as she tried to explain what caused her son to stray from his good upbringing and travel the path of personal destruction right back to the ghetto.

"I'm not sure what caused it," she lamented. "Maybe it was his peers. Maybe it was the divorce from his father. He was only three years old when I divorced his dad, but I think children sense a natural connection to their biological parent. We've tried treatment programs and family therapy. His main problem is that he is in denial about his substance abuse. He doesn't seem to believe that it's serious enough to destroy his life."

The quest for the ultimate high is a potent force in America. Drug abuse and addiction cast a wide pall over all those affected. Drugs destroy lives and wreak havoc on families and communities. Caught up in a network of deceit, drug users steal to support their habits, lie to cover their tracks, risk loss of personal relationships, and forsake God and all others to sustain their habits. Public awareness of the devastation of drug use—both legal and illegal—has produced only minimal success in curbing public desire. The nation's drug czar seems powerless. Local law enforcement officials are rendered impotent. And in some areas, illegal drug dealing has taken over the entire community.

TERRI'S CHALLENGE

Terri left Atlanta because of the sharp decline in her living standards. She was also attempting to reclaim her life after more than a decade of wild self-discovery that led to her poly-drug abuse. Terri was an experimenter. She had tried it all, but was partial toward amphetamines, marijuana, alcohol, and cocaine. Being back home would offer her the safe haven that she needed to recover.

"My memories of my small community didn't include drugs," she states. "I can't ever say that I recalled men standing around selling or doing drugs. But things were different when I got back."

Terri wanted to change her life. In 1982, she returned to Alabama, moved in with her grandparents, and assumed a care-taker role. Terri was an unemployed mother with a young child. She knew that she would qualify for welfare, but was cognizant of the fact that public assistance payments in Alabama were notoriously low. Welfare funds simply were not enough.

Terri returned to school at the local community college in continued pursuit of the bachelor's degree. Pharmacy was no longer an option, but being a schoolteacher was still within the realm of possibility. There she met Hasam, nine years her junior, but persistent in his efforts to woo her into a serious relationship. She resisted for some time, but finding no other takers, Terri accepted his interest as genuine and freed herself to pursue a love affair with the young student.

She served as the experienced teacher and mentor. Terri told stories of a life far more worldly than anything her young lover had ever experienced. They studied together, laughed together, made frequent love, shared baby-sitting responsibility, and got high together. After a year of passion, they decided to marry. Terri filed for divorce from her first husband and married Hasam as soon as the divorce was final.

For the next several years, Terri and Hasam struggled to maintain a decent quality of life. Two additional children were added to the family. Terri's grandparents died, leaving their home to Terri and Hasam. Drugs were part of the everyday experience. They knew all the drug dealers in the community and the dealers knew them. They both thought about kicking the habit. At one point, extended family members threatened to take custody of the three children if they did not seek help for their problem. Terri recalled:

"My family put me in a treatment facility for substance abuse. They portrayed it like a vacation. They said that the place had swimming pools and things like that. My sisters came over to the house and picked up the children. My husband, my mother, and his mother took care of them. My husband was abusing just as much, but he had a better handle on things.

"I was in one program for twenty-eight days. Then I went to another. It was a more public kind of thing. There was something about my insurance running out and not wanting to pay for the other facility.

"It was mostly the drink that forced me to go in, but I was also taking cocaine, marijuana, and any kind of pills that I could find.

"They told me that if I did not go into treatment that I wouldn't get my children back. I went. But as soon as I got out, I went right back to doing my thing."

Ten years had passed since Terri returned home from Atlanta. At forty, she was a mature woman with three active children. She and Hasam had been married for nine years. During one difficult period, they separated. It didn't last long. When they reunited, they talked about having a fourth child.

Terri and Hasam struggled to manage their day-to-day affairs. They were responsible and productive citizens during the day and regular drug users in the evenings and on the weekends. Nothing else seemed to work, and nothing else seemed to matter.

JUDITH'S CHALLENGE

For the most part, Judith's exposure to drugs and drug abuse was limited to what she read in books and what she saw on television. She wasn't totally naive. Obviously there were people in the community who were drug users, but she was shielded from this harsh reality when she returned home to her comfortable middle-class environment. Moreover, Judith never understood the attraction. She worshiped her body as a temple and couldn't imagine abusing it with drugs.

Judith's life as a blissful wonder left little to be desired. Her son had matured into a fine young man of whom she was extremely proud. She was a high-powered public administrator who was greatly admired by friends and peers. Certainly, there were a few ups and downs, but nothing that caused her any major concern. She was stunned when she discovered that her husband of fifteen years had turned to drugs.

"I was never a very wild person," Judith explained. "I tried drugs once. It was Hawaiian Gold. It put a bubble in my throat and scared me half to death. The experience freaked me out so bad I taped it. I asked God to please get me through this experience. I would never ever touch anything illegal again.

"My husband was different. He started hanging out drinking and smoking dope. It was a challenge to me and to our relationship. He said that he would stop drinking and smoking other stuff. He has to work on it. Right now, he likes to say that he is under construction."

"Under construction" might be the phrase that is used by several of these sisters as they talk about problems of substance abuse in their families. They were most disheartened when their children, husbands, or lovers had fallen victim to drug abuse, although sisters, brothers, aunts, and uncles were also affected. Cocaine and crack were identified as the most despised substances as the women talked about the difficulty in overcoming this modern-day addiction.

For many of the women, memories of their fathers' abusive drinking habits were also painful. They were alcoholics during a period when hard drinking was a very socially acceptable activity for men. As these women reflected on their childhood years, most were willing to concede that their fathers were victims of racial discrimination. Their manhood was constantly challenged. As African American men, they never had the opportunity to maximize all of their potential. Their dreams were crushed by the social restrictions placed on the African American community throughout the greater part of the twentieth century. Unfortunately, too many died before they had the opportunity to turn their lives around.

DEATH COMES CALLING

Forty-six-year-old Evelyn had made a successful move from the ghetto to the suburbs. She was a government worker with years of seniority on her side, and didn't want to be reminded of the perils of poverty and ghetto life.

Evelyn fought frequently with her brothers about their drug use. Now that they were gone, she mourned their loss and regretted how they had spent their time together.

Death is the natural end to the life cycle, but its untimely arrival is a major social disruption. As we age, the angel of death becomes a more frequent visitor and shatters our illusions of optimal health and perpetual longevity.

With a current life expectancy of 66.9 years, black males are often the first to die. Black males between ages 15 and 25 are at the greatest risk for homicide and suicide. Coupled with cancer, coronary artery disease, hypertension, stroke, and other social and physical threats, the average black male barely lives long enough to collect social security. Black women fare far better. Life expectancy for black females is 75.2 years—exactly 5 years shorter than their white female counterparts. There is one exception to the rule. If black males or females reach age 80 or beyond, the black-white crossover effect asserts itself. As they move toward the century mark, the black mortality rate is lower than that of whites.

Black/white discrepancies in heath status and longevity rates impact the lives of sisters. Black women experience the loss of their fathers and male counterparts at a much earlier age than white women. Kalilah was only eight years old when her father died. Ayanna was sixteen when her father passed away from problems associated with acute alcoholism. Chrystal's father, who so enjoyed his one and only vice of smoking cigarettes, developed lung cancer when he was fifty-eight. Cancer claimed his life at sixty.

In her early forties, Nashea lost her father after a long battle against cancer. Shortly thereafter, she lost her younger brother to AIDS. Ayanna was thirty-six when she watched her closest friend wither away from a disease called sarcoidosis. He was only thirty-four. And it seems that almost everyone had a story about a friend, family member, or close neighbor who had lost someone to gang or drug-related violence.

Sisters, too, are lost to premature death. Roslyn was only seven, but she vividly recalls the turmoil that followed the death of her mother, who died from complications associated with lupus. When Darla was forty-one, her sixty-five-year-old mother died from complications associated with diabetes. At the time of the interview, Tea was still mourning the loss of her mother from heart disease that had occurred four years earlier. But several of the more poignant stories came from sisters who told of the pain and grief that accompanied the loss of close sister friends and how they chose to die alone.

Juanita is a forty-two-year-old media consultant. Her parents are both alive and well and live comfortably in a suburban community in Waldorf, Maryland. As an only child from a very small extended family, she has never been faced with the personal trauma associated with the loss of a family member. However, she described the loss of her close friend as one of the more troubling emotional experiences of midlife.

"I can't begin to describe how I feel," she stated, still teary-eyed as she attempted to relay the story. "I know some people die young, but not those close to you. We had been close friends since high school. She was only forty-one and died from some disease that black people usually don't suffer from. I can't even tell you what it was. I was so totally unprepared for the call. She never told me she was sick. I would see her in church from time to time. She started to look thin, but I thought that it was her new diet. She never said she was dying. And I couldn't see it. I was so angry. I felt like I had been denied the opportunity to provide her support and comfort. I wondered what kind of friend she thought I was. Why wasn't she willing to share her pain, fear, and sorrows with me? I know we're supposed to be strong, but I'll never understand what kind of strength is needed to suffer alone in your final hours."

I felt pretty much the same way when Belinda died. Belinda and I had always remained in touch with one another following our graduation from Cabrini College. We were the only two who had made it out of a starting line of eleven inner-city black females who were offered full scholarships to attend the college. Our friendship was forged out of necessity. We stuck together like glue while we were in college, determined to make it through. Our lives went in separate directions once we graduated.

Belinda was a high school teacher for the Philadelphia Archdiocese. I was a professor at a predominantly white state college in southern New Jersey. She was a deeply religious, mild-mannered integrationist. I was a radical black cultural nationalist who frequently described God as a dashiki-wearing, dark-skinned brother with a medium-sized afro. She married a white man. Twice I married a black man. Belinda celebrated Christmas and I celebrated Kwanzaa.

When I had not heard from her in two years, I assumed that we both were storing up our good memories to share at our upcoming twenty-fifth college reunion. I was so looking forward to it. I was devastated when I got the call informing me of Belinda's death. For more than two years she had endured a slow, painful demise, her body ravaged by a blood disorder that sucked the life out of every vessel and organ. Yet she never told me that she was dying. She suffered in silence. Belinda's death left me grieving inconsolably at the mass for Christian burial. And I, too, had lingering questions about friendship and what it meant to die alone.

Accepting death, grief, pain, and suffering is part of the midlife passage. Sisters had to come to grips with thoughts of their own mortality, as they often were confronted with the premature death of family and friends. Moreover, the failing health status of many of their aging parents forced them to recognize that this, too, would ultimately lead to their demise.

Darlene is a fifty-one-year-old educational administrator. She has her moment every morning when she gets out of bed "and my arthritis starts to talk to me when I put my foot on the floor." She maintains a mental picture of herself as a vibrant, young woman. "Sometimes when I look in the mirror," she muses, "I question why that old-looking gray-haired woman is in there impersonating me."

While Darlene shares a joyous and satisfying life with her husband and twelve-year-old son, she becomes despondent when she thinks about how little time she has left to spend with her seventy-five-year-old mother.

"I would say that it is the one thing that saddens me the most. She has moved up here with me and I'm close enough to visit her every day. But she is getting old and her health is failing. She has five or six different ailments and is on all kinds of medication. I know that she will not be with me much longer."

The time she has left may, indeed, be limited. And Darlene wants to give her mother as much of herself as possible before it is too late. "So when the time comes," she adds, "I can feel good about the good times that we shared."

SURVIVING DIVORCE

Whereas some significant social relationships are terminated by death, others are ended voluntarily. Friends and social acquaintances of the sisters with whom I spoke whose relationships proved to be disruptive and limiting were discarded. As sisters matured struggling to maintain relationships fraught with social gossip, personal tensions, and petty jealousies seemed far less worthy of their valuable time. Moreover, sisters were forced to distance themselves from family members whose antisocial behaviors were strangling and potentially threatening to their own social stability and well-being. But by far, the greatest voluntary separations were caused by divorce, which was more like a social death. And divorce is a major social disruption in the lives of black women.

Divorce has a negative impact on all women. The family's economic status declines significantly when the male leaves the home, generally taking with him the larger share of the family income. Child support payments are beneficial, if you manage to get paid. The National Center for Child Support reports that fewer than 50 percent of those ordered to pay child support fulfill their court-ordered obligations. Alimony, which in the past helped many women maintain their standard of living, diminished with the change in divorce laws and social customs. By the 1980s, women were expected to earn their own income, and many had demonstrated their ability to do so.

CHRYSTAL'S CHALLENGE

For thirty-five-year-old Chrystal, divorce was the most destructive force in her life. After thirteen years of marriage, she knew it was time to move on. She was no longer the innocent twenty-two-year-old who felt that marriage and children were necessary to make her a complete woman. She had been transformed into a confident, intelligent, sophisticated woman who had a better appreciation of what she wanted out of life. However, she faced a dilemma: Would she sacrifice her own personal growth and development to maintain the marriage?

Chrystal's husband was a decent hardworking man who was beginning to struggle with his own midlife crisis. All of his life he had dreamed of being an artist. From his point of view, he missed his opportunity to do so when he committed himself to marriage and a business career at the age of twenty-four. As Chrystal's own professional career goals started to take shape, he became more and more confused about his own needs. He was not an abusive husband. There was no evidence of infidelity. Chrystal had never been unfaithful during their marriage and lusted for no one. Quite frankly, they no longer had anything in common, except their eleven-year-old daughter. Chrystal decided to terminate the marriage.

The divorce was difficult. Vague descriptions from both partners citing irreconcilable differences didn't garner much support or sympathy from friends and family on either side. Often, they were met with queries about the benefits of marital counseling. But, according to Chrystal, it was not a relationship worth saving.

Following her divorce, Chrystal considered dating. But what were her options? Divorced people are part of the walking wounded. Many come with heavy baggage, and finding new lovers and forming new partnerships can be difficult when festering wounds from previous relationships have not yet healed. Where would Chrystal find mature, single black men? Were women in midlife still attractive enough to gain a brother's interest? What risks were involved in the dating game? Was celibacy a good choice? The questions were abundant, but the answers elusive. And these issues were hotly debated wherever sister friends gathered.

AYANNA'S CHALLENGE

When Ayanna entered her thirties, she began to find liberation as a single-parent professional. Her nine-year marriage had ended, and, as she predicted, her former husband started to drift away from her life. Child visitations were infrequent, and efforts to collect the promised child support payments led to hostility and turmoil. Her efforts to elicit the support of the family court are summarized as "the nightmare at 1801 Vine Street." Fortunately, her educational training and professional position provided her with a sufficient income to keep the family out of poverty.

Ayanna deeply regretted the loss that her children experienced in their father's absence, but she was powerless to do anything about it. She thought about the possibility of starting over with a new partner.

She had engaged in many discussions with her sister friends about attracting a new mate. They were unanimous in their opinion: What awaits you in the world of dating is a vast wasteland! Moreover, the idea of exposing her children to "some stranger" was unappealing. Other sisters who talked about dating and starting new relationships shared this concern. Who was Mommy's new friend? Should we call him Uncle Bob, Uncle Jay, or Uncle John? And how many "uncles" were you allowed to introduce to your children before it was considered scandalous?

There were other pressing questions about possible outcomes if the relationship continued to develop: Was it best to spend the night at his place, away from your kids, or should he spend his nights with you and the kids? Was marriage a possibility? Would a new husband or lover accept the children? Horror stories about the negative impact of boyfriends and stepfathers on children from previous relationships were plentiful. Some were outrageously exaggerated myths. Unfortunately, others proved to be quite accurate.

TARA'S CHALLENGE

Tara is a dynamic and confident affirmative action baby. She was born in Detroit, Michigan, in 1955. She married young and had two children in her early twenties. The relationship was extremely abusive. Like Kalilah, she fled her home, clinging to her children and taking only her personal belongings. She recalled, "I was trying to feed my two-year-old. The baby was on my hip. My husband put a gun to my head and told me to jump out of the window. I asked him if I could take the baby to the bathroom first. He said yes. I slipped out of the front door and never went back. I moved to another state. I had nothing."

Tara spent several years on welfare trying to pull herself together. She returned to college to upgrade her skills and prepare for a career change in a higher-paying field. Prior to the era of welfare reform, women could enroll in college courses and seek undergraduate degrees as they prepared themselves to leave the welfare rolls. However, following the implementation of the federal welfare reform laws under the Clinton administration, this option has all but been eliminated under current guidelines. But Tara was able to remain in school, collect public assistance, and care for her two children without any permanent family disruption. She completed her studies in two and a half years and went searching for a professional position.

Free of welfare and eager to start a new life, Tara landed a plum job in the aerospace industry through a government-sponsored affirmative action program. It was the opportunity she had been waiting for. Tara was extremely motivated. She utilized every available talent and skill that she could muster to make certain that she performed at maximum peak. Her dedication to excellence and exceptional job performance were rewarded with salary upgrades and promotion to the supervisory ranks.

Tara met Jose by accident. He was a tenant in her apartment building. Jose was a gorgeous male specimen. She was fascinated by his charm and captivating personality. He flashed a bright smile and tossed numerous pleasantries her way. He appeared younger—maybe about five years—and was of Hispanic origin. They enjoyed an intense and exclusive dating arrangement before they finally decided to marry less than a year after their first date.

It appeared to be a good marriage that lasted for sixteen years. They worked on his educational and career goals together. Although Jose was an illegal alien from South America when they first met, Tara assisted him in gaining citizenship. Eventually, mounting tensions in the marriage helped Tara to focus on her spiritual needs as she turned to the church for guidance. To strengthen her faith, she wanted the entire family to join the church. After sixteen years of marriage, she wanted to do all that she could to keep the family together.

But the marriage ended abruptly when Tara discovered that Jose had molested her oldest daughter. Fearful that the revelation of sexual misconduct would destroy the family, it was a secret that her daughter had kept to herself for many years. For

Tara, it was one of the most heart-wrenching, devastating discoveries of her life. She was totally oblivious to what was going on in her own home, and it was troubling. Why was she so blindly in love? Was she guilty of parental neglect? The divorce was swift and immediate. However, the guilt lingered, a constant reminder of her failings as a mother and protector of her offspring. How could she find a way to uplift herself from the depth of depression and despair that presently engulfed her life?

At this time in her life, it was hard to imagine that there could be a turnaround anytime soon. She had to build her world all over again.

SISTER WISDOM

There are powerful, complex forces in the social and physical environment that can work against a black woman's ability to achieve a satisfying life at any stage. Negotiating successful passage can be difficult. Sisters' experiences with this phase of life have taught them the following lessons:

- *Don't blame yourself for other's actions.* Don't accept responsibility for things over which you have no control. This only adds unnecessary stress to your life. Invest in your children when they are young. Provide structure and guidance. Give as much as you can to those who are willing to listen and take your advice. Ultimately, you can only accept responsibility for your own behavior.

- *There is no hiding place from reality.* You can come in from the storm, but it may be difficult to shield yourself and your family from social problems experienced by the larger community. We are products of our environment. Protecting your family and yourself against major social problems is an ongoing challenge.

- *You can survive divorce and single parenthood.* Once you've made the decision to end your marriage (which is often the most difficult part), reprioritize your life and cast yourself in the role of a single competent woman. Believe in your ability to do what is necessary to raise self-confident, productive children. Never equate single parenthood with failure. Quickly finding a replacement lover should be the least of your concerns.

- *Revisit the writing on the wall: II.* More often than not, there are telltale signs of destructive behaviors. Don't ignore early warning signals. At the first sign of abuse, seek help. At the first sign of violence, get out.

- *Savor the good times; death comes sooner than expected.* Losing a loved one is inevitable. Never hesitate to be the first to say, "I love you." Express your concern for those who are close to you.

- *When watching the craziness of other, don't go crazy, too.* When facing your darkest hour, remain positive about the outcome. Take the time you need to work things out. Seek professional help if needed.

Keep a copy of Gloria Gaynor's empowering hit "I Will Survive" within reach.

As we reflect on this stage of development, it is striking to see how often black women encounter major stumbling blocks that they must confront and resolve with courage. Roslyn struggles to save her son from the devastation of substance abuse, while Terri and her husband can't seem to function without a daily excursion into the world of drugs. Judith, too, struggles to rescue her husband from the lure of the streets and the pleasures of a fast high. Tara, having survived an abusive first marriage, struggles with the guilt and shame that manifested itself after the betrayal of her second spouse. And divorce has, temporarily, derailed both Chrystal and Ayanna.

Happy endings don't appear in the middle of life's script for even the most resilient black women. Sisters must be tenacious in their efforts to find satisfying lives. For those who might want to argue with this bleak view, there is the evidence to the contrary. And they would have a point. Consider Darla: nothing seemed to get in the way of Darla's happiness.

6

Can We Just Turn Back the Hands of Time?

I n the midst of her continuing give and take with her family's issues and her own unfinished business of her late thirties and forties, a black woman needs to prepare for the physical and psychological challenges that come with maturity. Her self-image is likely to take a severe hit. If she has not resolved her childhood struggle with sensitive issues of attractiveness, beauty, and desirability, episodes of midlife fright can produce unexpected consequences. However, midlife can also provide opportunities for renewed self-awareness.

CLINGING TO THAT YOUTHFUL LOOK

Have you ever experienced a moment in your life when you suddenly realized that you were just not as young as you used to be? I know I have. I was preparing to do a solo dance performance at a local recital. I had been performing for more than twenty-five years, and stepping out onto the stage was no big deal. Thirty seconds into the presentation, I realized that I wasn't going to make it to the end of the dance. I was breathing hard, my heart was beating fast, and I was suffering from exhaustion. I was completely out of shape, and, at that very moment, realized that I was way past my performance prime. What was I thinking? I ran to the side of the stage, grabbed an empty chair, flopped my butt on the seat, and started to improvise. I was going to save face any way that I could.

It's periodic moments like this that cause you to stop for a moment of reflection and introspection. You recognize that changes are occurring. And whatever you had planned or hoped to accomplish in life, now is the time to move forward. Chrystal also remembers her moment quite well.

"I was shopping at Macy's department store for that special little outfit to attend my girlfriend's wedding. I remember chuckling to myself quite often because I couldn't believe that she was finally getting married. Seemed to me like she was searching all of her life. At forty-two, I know that she was thrilled to find the man of her dreams. I hadn't yet met the man, and I thought the wedding was happening too fast. I remember joking to myself that he probably just asked her last night. But it was a special occasion and I wanted to look good.

"I was already feeling some level of frustration because nothing seemed to fit. I tried on every size seven in the junior shop, but nothing seemed quite right. I wasn't about to try on a size nine, because that wasn't me. Finally, I decided that

Macy's just wasn't as upscale as it used to be and headed toward Lord and Taylor's.

"As I got off the escalator, I was lured to the counter by the sweet smell of jasmine. I couldn't resist sampling the bottles of perfume. It was then I overheard a young girl about the age of thirteen say to her mother, 'That's a good-looking old lady. I hope I look like that when I get old.' I looked around several times to see the old lady before I realized that she was talking about me. I couldn't believe it. Suddenly I was middle-aged and I wasn't ready for it. And why was I still shopping in the junior shop at Macy's?"

For other women, this moment of truth comes earlier.

> I don't know how old I was when I first started to feel like I was no longer a young woman. I think it was some time in my late thirties. I guess it sorta just creeps up on you. When I was about twenty-nine, I was sitting in a bar, allowing men to buy me drinks. Once I knew I had consumed too much, I started to refuse their offers. An old guy in his fifties took offense. "You know, you ain't exactly a spring chicken!" he hollered over in my direction. "I am too a spring chicken," I wanted to shout back, but I didn't. He was just a drunk old man. But several years later, I remember walking down the street and noticing that the men were not hollering. When did the men stop hollering?
>
> —*Debbie, age 42*

Over and over again, sisters cited weight gain as a sign of their awareness of their changing self-image. For some, adding a few pounds was not an issue.

"If it's there, it must be because it belongs where it is," one sister said. "I don't get on the scale and don't know how much I weigh." For this confident sister and many others like her, curvaceous bodies are preferred to skinny ones. Waif images do not offer sensual appeal.

Fitness gurus suggest that a cardiovascular workout at least three times a week is good for the heart. A consistent approach to exercise also holds the promise of reducing your weight and altering your dress size. A sharp reduction in caloric intake promises much of the same. Thus, sisters frequently make promises to themselves to "change my diet and start exercising so that I can look good and feel better."

For some women, the new healthy regime starts on Monday, begins to falter by Wednesday, and completely falls by the wayside on the weekend. Undaunted, a new promise is made on Sunday night to get back to the program on Monday. It is a vicious cycle for some, but others manage to stick with their fitness programs for months or years. Their victorious attempts at maintaining a rigorous exercise and diet schedule are motivated by concerns for health and physical appearance. Sisters expressed their belief that physically fit women project a youthful image.

Nashea does not want to move up to another dress size. "I get up at 5 A.M. every morning to do my exercise. I buy fashionable clothes and use facial creams and makeup to help maintain my youthful looks."

At fifty-three, Gaynell is a seasoned community development specialist who enjoys her work and the time she spends traveling around the country to evaluate local initiatives.

Though married to the same man for thirty years, she's best described as an independent free floater who indulges her every want and desire. She acknowledges that she "weighs too much," but has no immediate plans to tackle the problem. Wanting to project a youthful image is another matter.

"Every day I do something to try and make myself look younger," she confidently states. "I wear braids, I dye my hair, I wear Afrocentric clothing, and wear plenty of makeup and Afrocentric jewelry. I'm going to continue to do what I do and look good while I'm doing it."

Just the sight of strands of gray hair frightens Tea and forces her to spring into immediate action. "I started to gray, rather rapidly, in my early forties. I just wasn't ready for it. I started to color my hair back then and will continue to do so. I wish I had invested my money in Dark and Lovely stock. I'd be rich by now."

Forty-four-year-old Jasmine feels the same way: "When I turned forty, I decided to lock my hair as a gift to myself. That's when I noticed it was turning gray. I could not envision myself as a gray-haired woman. I started to dye my hair a burnished red-brown color that I always wished I had. I've been dyeing my locks every other month for the last three years."

Jocelyn is a social worker who just turned fifty. "I wish I had taken better care of myself," she states. "I ate too much junk food. I didn't eat properly and I never exercised. Now, I'm paying the price. I have high cholesterol and a blocked artery. But I still try to project myself as a young person. I walk fast. I think older people walk slowly. I have friends who are younger than me. I think that keeps you feeling young."

Forty-eight-year-old Jerri is a tall, fair-complexioned sister with short blonde hair. She works part-time as an accountant. Jerri has been happily married for twenty-five years. She has three children and a two-story colonial home in an upscale, bucolic suburban community. The family is financially set with a bright future. Positive memories of her youth provide a constant source of inspiration.

"In my house, I create an illusion. I have pictures all over of when I was young and when I looked my best. I get out of bed in the morning and I see this gorgeous young woman posing in a white pants suit. I say to myself, 'That's me.' It doesn't matter that it's not me now—it used to be me. I wouldn't dare go out of the house in a white pants suit."

"I go out dancing on the weekend" is how Muriel describes the way she attempts to stay fit. Muriel is a forty-seven-year-old mother of three who struggles with obesity. Dancing not only reminds her of her youth, but also offers a rigorous form of exercise as she recaptures the old cha-cha and crossfire dance steps that she used to do "way back in the sixties." "I have to stay in bed all day Sunday to recover," she adds, "but the dancing reminds me of what I used to do when I was younger."

Forty-three-year-old Vera shares an experience common to many women in their middle years. Many sisters will identify with her story. Vera is a professor of education. She is a single parent with two children in college.

"I went to my twenty-fifth high school reunion just last month," she recalls. "You know how you definitely want to look good. I dieted for months before the dinner to try and get back into shape. I didn't look bad, but I was not the size 7 that

I was when I left high school. I went down to Nordstrom's Department Store to buy an outfit. While I was there, I stopped in the lingerie department. I must have purchased every spandex undergarment available. The slip, the bra, the panties, and the panty hose all had some Lycra substance to hide the additional rolls of fat that had formed under my arms, on my waist, and around my hips, butt, and thighs.

"I walked into the banquet hall with my head high in my size 12 black dress with all the spandex holding me in. I could hardly breathe all night, but it was worth the price. People kept telling me how good I looked. They lied. Almost all the women wore black. Everybody was trying to hide their bulging middle-aged bodies. I could get through the night, but there is no way I'd try to pull it off on an everyday basis."

Carla, the Hampton graduate, didn't quite realize that time had passed by. Often, the subtleties of aging are imperceptible and you don't recognize the changes until long after the body has been altered.

"I went shopping at the thrift shop to see what I could pick up," recalls Carla of her special moment of recognition. "Rich white women discard their designer goods for the purpose of charity or whatever, and sometimes you can get a real good deal. I saw this form-fitting polka dot dress with puff sleeves, low-cut neckline, and a bow in the back. The material and design were perfect. It was just my size and everything about the dress said, 'this is me.' It was such an inexpensive bargain, I took it home without trying it on.

"I thought I would wear the dress that night. I was going out on a date and I was going to look good. I remember putting it on and looking in the mirror. It reminded me of a scene from the movie *Whatever Happened to Baby Jane*. I looked absolutely foolish. *Gone are the days*, I thought to myself. That dress was perfect for a young woman, and I was no longer one of them."

Ayanna's solution to turning back the hands of time is quite simple. "I put on a red dress with spaghetti straps and go out clubbing. There's not a self-respecting brother in Philly who doesn't respond to a sister in a red dress."

Clubbing is, indeed, a youthful activity. For me, it conjures up images of loud music, smoke-filled rooms, and the smell of fried foods and perspiration all mixed into one. But for Chrystal it represented something far less desirable.

"When I was in my late thirties, my girlfriend and I went out on a Saturday night to the Peppermint Lounge. I'm certain that we both got all dolled up because we were still single and didn't have any real good prospects on the horizon. I knew that we had made a mistake the moment that we pulled up to the front of the club. The place was overflowing with a bunch of young kids. I felt like somebody's mother. We both sat down at the bar and ordered drinks. Why were we in here? Were we waiting for somebody to pick us up? It had to be one of my less dignified moments. I never wanted to go bar-hopping or clubbing after that."

GETTING MYSELF FIXED

Rachel is a thirty-seven-year-old public health nurse. When black moles first showed up on her neck, she wasted little time in going to the dermatologist to get herself "de-moled." "I couldn't take it," she said. "The doctor went up one side and down the other. It hurt, but I looked a lot better. They tell me that these things grow back. But I'll do it as often as possible to keep my neck clear."

There was very little talk of plastic or cosmetic surgery as a method to alter facial appearance or to reshape the body into something more beautiful. Among the many sisters who I talked to in great detail, only one admitted to having any form of cosmetic surgery. Jocelyn, who walks fast so that people will know that she is still a young person, shares her experience with reconstructive surgery.

"After I had my second child, I couldn't get rid of the pregnant belly. I was so bothered by this. I was thirty-three years old and thought that my figure was unsightly. I went under the knife for a tummy tuck. It's not something that I would do again. I suffer from keloids, and the surgery left a big scar. I have good genes. I look younger than my fifty years. My face is smooth. I have beautiful skin. I don't think I'll ever need a face-lift."

The fear of keloids may be a reason why black women are cautious in considering plastic surgery as a youth-enhancing option. According to leading dermatologists, people with darker skin tones are much more likely to suffer from problems with keloids than their fair-skin counterparts. Translation: White people fair best under the surgeon's knife! However, more and more sisters are opting for plastic surgery. The most popular procedure is liposuction.

Another explanation for the lack of interest by sisters in cosmetic surgery is that people with darker skin tones do not suffer as severely from the effects of sun damage. Moreover, skin cancers, often caused by the damaging effect of overexposure to the sun, are far more prevalent among whites than blacks.

Sharon, a schoolteacher in Jackson, Mississippi, is only forty-three years old, but she is bothered by the deep crease in her forehead. She remembers how youthful she looked before the wrinkle made her forehead its permanent home. "I've considered using cosmetic surgery to get rid of the line in the middle of my forehead. Then I thought about how frivolous that was and decided not to be bothered. I accept who I am."

As Jessica entered the middle phase, she finally found the courage and the resources to address an issue that she had felt strongly about since childhood. "I don't know if it's turning back the hands of time," she giggled, "but when I turned forty, I decided to get braces. It's something that I've wanted to do for a long time: Fix this gap in my teeth!"

YOUTHFUL IMAGINATIONS, AGING BODIES

Daphne is a forty-eight-year-old grandmother of three. She is employed as a civil service worker at the local government complex. Daphne doesn't worry about turning back the hands of time. She has never viewed herself as a middle-aged woman. "I don't think physical age matters," she insists. "It's all in your mind. I'm not going to act like an older woman because I don't see myself that way. I do the same kinds of things that young people do. I go out to clubs, I take dance classes and perform when I have the opportunity.

My boyfriend is sixteen years younger than me. We've been together for three years."

Valerie is a forty-one-year-old attorney in Chicago. When asked about the things that she does to help her turn back the hands of time, she laughed hauntingly and responded, "Child, I still smoke weed!"

Finally, sisters like Olivia, Roslyn, and Shelli expressed sentiments that suggested they were still too young to tell stories about the way things used to be. However, all conceded that they missed the soul-stirring, old school classic sounds of the eighties and the funky, freaky-deek dance craze associated with their youth.

One of the great joys of midlife is simply getting there. As the sisters in this book matured, they gained a greater appreciation for the wonders of the human body. Physical changes are inevitable. None of us are the way we used to be. Eventually, the body will show signs of aging, and sisters must learn to adapt. However, too many sisters have neglected their own health needs and physical appearance as they have focused their attention on the needs of children, spouses, and parents. Midlife signals a time for change. With much greater resolve, sisters must commit themselves to seeking answers and solutions to their own health issues and concerns.

SISTERPAUSE

Sisterpause is how I describe the socially confounding and physically confusing state of rapidly depleting hormonal activity in our middle stage of life. For black women, the sisterpause offers a midlife lesson in incongruency. On the one hand, we sense the internal biological changes occurring within our bodies. On the other hand, our outward appearance continues to send us the message that we are still fairly young and good-looking. It is this image of a youthful persona that we struggle to maintain, even as we experience perimenopause, the beginning of the passage through menopause itself.

Somehow, your mothers and grandmothers never told you that the sisterpause was coming. The secrecy that surrounds the sisterpause is second only to the hidden secrets about sexual intercourse and pregnancy prevention that no one wanted to talk about until after the fact. The "change" came to our aunts and mothers, but it was a silent visitor. Those maternal figures willing to broach the subject with us or with each other generally discussed natural ways to get through it. Garden herbs and natural teas were the answer to physiological changes that "older" women experienced, including night sweats and daytime fanning. And now we are those older women.

The current generation of midlifers is much more enlightened about the natural changes and rhythms of the body. Information is a powerful tool against ignorance. Why, then, was the coming of the sisterpause a surprise to many black women? As part of the rabble-rousing, age-defying baby-boomer generation, did we really believe that menopause was never going to happen to us? Since we firmly believed that we were in better shape than black women of the previous generation, and since we viewed menopause as an "old lady condition," it is as if we believed it couldn't arrive until we were well past our prime. And whatever the symptoms, we would seek a cure. There were new scientific ways to delay the inevitable process.

In conversation many sisters strike a defiant pose. "I refuse to fan myself in public," one sister told me. Another stated, "At the first sign of menopause, I'm going to the doctor and tell him to give me my goddamn estrogen! I refuse to break out in a sweat."

Quietly, several sisters indicated that they had slipped into a perimenopausal state at an early age. "I started quite early, in my late thirties," was how one sister responded. "After the doctor confirmed what was going on, I changed my diet and my routine right away. I work out every day and watch my weight. I've decided against taking hormonal replacement treatment. It's too risky for black women. I'm going to fight this thing as long as I can."

Other sisters told of their astonishment when informed by their physicians of the onset of menopause. Janet is a fifty-eight-year-old public service worker. She started to go through the change at the age of thirty-six. "I was shocked," she states. "I've never really heard of anyone starting menopause at that age. I don't know what my mother went through because we never talked about it. I don't really know if it was normal or not. But by the time I turned forty-five, it was all over."

Martha was forty-three when she started to miss periods. Fearful that she was pregnant again, she quickly visited her gynecologist. "When he told me that I was going through menopause, I didn't believe it. I had been pregnant twice before, but ended both pregnancies. How could I be going through menopause?"

NEW HEALTH THREATS

While the medical statistics do not indicate that black women are more likely to receive hysterectomies than white women or other women of color, many sisters felt that this was indeed the case. They all knew sisters who had one. The disappearance of black female uteruses, in all regions of the country, was attributed to the uncontrollable growth of fibroid tumors.

Other serious medical situations are also becoming common among among sister friends. Judith's story is one example.

Judith's struggle with her husband's substance abuse problems exacted an emotional and financial toll. When her health started to fail, she attributed much of her decline to stress. Physical examination revealed something else: breast cancer. It would present her with one of her major life challenges. And she was not alone.

Tara, who quickly divorced her husband once she discovered that he had sexually molested her daughter, had just started to recover from her ordeal when she discovered that she, too, was suffering from breast cancer.

The fear of developing breast, cervical, or ovarian cancer is widely shared among black women. Early detection and treatment provide a crucial ray of hope for those who fall victim to these life-threatening but treatable illnesses.

MESSING WITH THE WRONG MEN

Just thinking about turning back the hands of time helped sisters to focus on things they wished they simply had not done. I must admit that I was somewhat surprised at the number of sisters who fessed up to having affairs with married men and several more who admitted to extramarital affairs. Who they are is not important. Their experiences and insights are relevant because they offer an additional perspective on black women. These sisters were willing to share secret details about their moments of sexual indiscretion because they believed that it might aid other sisters who are struggling with the same issues.

Generally, their involvement with married men occurred during their twenties and thirties. Their regrets came much later. Each sister had a slightly different take on how and why it happened.

"I started to feel like it was okay to see this married man," said one sister. "My girlfriend had been involved with a married guy for a few years and I was influenced by what she was doing. There was a whole crowd of people that supported this kind of behavior. I was single, as were all the other women. The married men were so attentive to all the sisters' needs. The guy I ended up having an affair with never promised me more than good sex and a good time. We were not thinking about falling in love and getting married.

"I stayed in the relationship for two years. I ended it because I was ready to move on to something more promising. But he did a lot for me. Not in a material sense, but in the level of emotional support that he provided. He encouraged me to pursue my dreams. He built up my level of confidence. He helped me to get back into school and finish my degree. I still have fond memories of the time we spent together even though, morally, I know it was not the right thing to do."

According to another, "Married men provided me with a certain degree of comfort in my development because I didn't have this great desire to get married and have a bunch of kids. What I did want was a man to warm my bed on a regular basis. And the right married men worked real hard to do that well because they couldn't do other things. So I don't have a problem with married men. You know, they could maintain the sanctity of their marriage, and I could do what I wanted. I was free to come and go as I pleased."

And another sister tells her story this way: "I accept full responsibility for what happened. I was lonely and desperate for companionship. He was playing the field. You start to find all kinds of ways to justify your behavior. I was thirty-three and old enough and mature enough to know better. We carried on for four months before it ended. He moved on to somebody else."

Several other women added the following insights and explanations:

"I didn't know that he was married. You make these dumb assumptions about people who are pursuing you. A married man wouldn't be bold enough to act this way in public, or so you think. It wasn't a confrontation with his wife that revealed his marital status and infidelity. It was a confrontation with his other girlfriend."

"I was young. He was young. It was lust more than anything else. The lying and cheating part was difficult on my relationship with my husband. In my own immature way, I think I did it to make certain that I was ready to end my marriage. I wanted to get caught. That way, he would have to leave me even if I didn't have the courage to do it."

"I'm a Christian woman. My grandmother and grandfather raised me. He [my grandfather] was a Methodist preacher. It's hard coming up with an explanation as to why it happened. We were both cheating on our spouses. Yes, it felt right at the time. It didn't last because making arrangements to meet him in the middle of the day was much too difficult. We probably spent a fortune on hotel rooms in the downtown area. It's much safer to be in a downtown hotel than a motel. You learn never to park your car outside a motel room.

"I know that you're going to think that this sounds strange, but I do feel like the affair strengthened my marriage. It's been over ten years now. I no longer think much about it and no longer feel guilty. But I will probably stay married to my husband until he dies."

"I was bowled over by passion. I still don't understand it. From the very first moment we met, we knew that we belonged together. I had never felt so strongly about a relationship in all of my life. I was emotionally strung out, cried all the time, and did everything that I could to purge myself of these deep feelings. Sure, I wish it had never happened. Who would deliberately fall in love with someone who already was committed to another woman? That's what your mind says, but your heart—it feels free to do its own thing."

"What I regret most is the amount of time I spent in a relationship that I never should have entered. You wish that you could go back and reclaim that lost time. It was so unfulfilling. And I stayed in it for nine years. I wasted all of that time dealing with that fool."

"I started to see married men after I decided that I didn't want to get married again. The first one was a good experience. He gave me what I needed and I sent him home. The second one gave me trichomoniasis. That ended it. And before I got started on the third one, I decided to send him back home to his wife. That's when I decided . . . no more married men for me."

It didn't require the experience of an extramarital affair for sisters to recognize that they had given too much of themselves to unloving, unproductive relationships. On the average, black women spend more time being single than white women. This leads to more dating opportunities and the increased possibility of ending up in mismatched partnerships. One sister said, "I wish I hadn't wasted so much time seeing so many men. I think it's pretty bad when you start counting up all of your sexual conquests and you realize that you don't have enough fingers." Another sister was not regretful of the number of partners that she had, but rather, "I wish I hadn't treated them so badly. I've dogged a lot of brothers."

Ignorance, stubbornness, and fear of the unknown is how one sister described her long-term, marital relationship: "I wish I had never married my husband," she said. "I wish someone had told me about self-esteem. I wished I had listened to my mother and aunt when they told me that my husband-to-be was a radical, uncontrollable, angry man. I wish I hadn't spent eighteen years of my life living in an abusive relationship. And instead of being in therapy to recover from not having any self-esteem . . . I don't mean low self-esteem, I mean zero self-esteem . . . I could be using that money to buy me another time-share."

REGRETS

There were missed opportunities in the educational and professional realms as well. Sisters had hoped for better preparation in primary and secondary school. This would have helped to place them on equal footing with the white community. Poor educational preparation, combined with the lack of adequate educational guidance, forced many sisters to play catch-up as they attempted to prepare themselves for new career opportunities. Some of them hoped for greater exposure to nontraditional careers. And while some felt that they were denied opportunities to pursue lucrative job possibilities, others lacked the courage to pursue their dreams. As one sister shared: "I didn't go to law school because I thought that it would threaten my husband and my marriage. We got divorced anyway. I never did get to be a lawyer."

Sisters also commented on the difference in attitudes toward financial planning and financial security between the sisters who lay claim to generation midlife and younger black women. Seasoned midlifers talked about the seemingly financial sophistication of their younger sisters. At the age of fifty-five, Sondra is already retired. After twenty-five years of working in the post office, she had had enough. She enjoys the freedom of being able to do whatever she wants to do. Early retirement "is not necessarily financially rewarding, but it allows me to spend time working on my own business venture." Sondra wanted to get started a lot sooner, but she didn't have the funds to support her lifestyle. She believes that the situation is much different for younger sisters: "These younger women talk about their stock options, their portfolios, their pension plans. I don't remember thinking or preparing for those kinds of things when I started working. They're a different generation of sisters, and I admire them for that. I wish I had had the opportunity to start planning for my retirement a lot sooner."

For those whose search focused on spiritual contentment, the time wasted in the devil's playground was a major regret. Faithful followers—and there are many—believe that they have discovered the path to righteousness. One sister sums up their views in this single comment: "I wish I had found my spiritual center at a much earlier time. This has given me so much direction in my life. I would be a much different person today if I had discovered God when I was in my twenties or thirties."

Finally, there are events in our early lives that have a profound and irrevocable impact. The philosophy that it is never too late to start all over again may be true in some arenas but not in others. Consider the story of one forty-five-year-old sister who has learned firsthand the irrevocable consequences of youthful decisions.

"If I could do it all over again, I wouldn't have had the abortion. At the time, it was the right thing to do. I was twenty-eight, single, and no longer interested in the baby's father. I remember how relieved I felt when it was all over. I was in pain, physically and emotionally. And I felt guilty. I had nightmares several days after the procedure was over. I tried to put it out of my mind and never gave it much thought until I entered my forties. That's when I started to realize that I would not have any children.

"I've resisted getting a hysterectomy because I kept hoping that my Prince Charming would come along and we could get married and have children. I always wanted kids. But my fibroids kept growing. I've gotten several opinions about what should be done. I'm going to have the operation in the spring. I've accepted that this is going to be my life, but the abortion is my deepest regret."

SISTER WISDOM

Can we just turn back the hands of time? Probably not. But moments of reflection provide sisters with valuable lessons about the past that helped shape their future. Keep in mind the following:

- *You know you shouldn't have done it, but it's too late to feel guilty now.* Everyone makes mistakes. If you feel like a sinner, pray for forgiveness. It will be given.
- *Define for yourself what looks and feels good.* There's no need to try to reclaim a twenty-year-old body, lifestyle, or mindset. Maturity comes with benefits. You no longer need to depend on others to validate your worth and dignity.
- *Health is one of your most prized possessions.* Make an aggressive attempt to monitor your health status. Start early in life. Medical treatments are available for a variety of ailments that plague black women.
- *Embrace your own youthful spirit.* If it feels good to you, it's good for you! That's what our elders used to say. Don't take yourself too seriously. Playfulness, humor, and fun can all be a part of the midlife experience.
- *If you plan on living, start planning for tomorrow.* It's never too late to set new goals for the future. Recreating memories of the good times provided brief moments of comic relief for these sisters. But midlife is about moving on; clinging to images of "the way we were" provided few tangible benefits. Reinvent yourself into "the woman who you want to be."

PART TWO

Our Pathways

7

Love and Happiness

I've worked in this job for sixteen years. I have all the skills and education that I need to take over and run this company. I'm already pretty close to the top in my division. Yet when they called me in last month and offered me the position of senior vice president, I wasn't able to respond. I kept thinking about the increase in salary and status. I thought about how I would be the envy of all my friends. And then I thought about my husband, my children, and my grandchildren . . . all still at home with me. How would this affect them? After struggling with it for a few days, I finally came to a decision. The promotion simply wasn't worth the sacrifices that I would be forced to make. I declined. And deep in my heart, I know that I did the right thing.

—Shirley, age 38

The ability to develop and maintain rewarding human relationships defines the pathways of the domestic warrior, single-parent professional, blissful wonder, and passionate soul mate. These sisters share much in common. They are nurturers, and they have found ways to nurture themselves as well as others. Sustained familial relationships have fueled their spirits and provided them with positive goals and direction. Some of their relationships were forged out of desire, others out of necessity.

In the women's movement, there is much discussion about women's role as nurturers and the burdens that go along with it. Some women resent nurturing responsibilities, feeling that their individual needs and desires must be suppressed in order to meet emotional, physical, and social needs of others. For these women, the acceptance of a traditional female role is simply not enough.

But for others, like the domestic warrior, placing the nurturing role at the very core of their existence shapes and defines them. It brings an abundance of joy and satisfaction. They are firmly anchored in the most traditional of female roles and the pleasures associated with home life. These sisters have located a comfortable space in the personal realm and are willing to make sacrifices to maintain competency in it.

ROSLYN'S PATHWAY

Roslyn's sense of joy and satisfaction in her current stage of life stems from the happiness that she garners from embracing the role as domestic warrior. It is what she wants to do and it is where she wants to be. But she cannot do it alone. It is a role that requires the cooperation and support of her husband. When Roslyn thinks about the problems and difficulties she encountered when attempting to add outside tasks to her domestic responsibilities, she has no qualms about the righteousness of her decision.

As a young woman, Roslyn felt overwhelmed by her changing social status, the responsibility to care for her children, and the burden of trying to resolve her own identity crisis. But not anymore. Midlife brought maturity, wisdom, and clarification of self. She is confident in her decision-making abilities and has assumed the role of domestic warrior by choice rather than chance.

"I know me. I know who I am," she insists. "I could not be satisfied with working, or being a student while trying to raise my children. You make decisions in life. And accepting my role as wife and mother means there are concessions. But I wouldn't do it any other way. You have less in some areas and more in others. My husband sometimes feels that he gets the short end of the stick, but there are times in your life when you have to give more to your children. He understands that.

"I spent a good deal of my time staying on top of my kids' needs. The amount of homework that is required of children today is not like it used to be. Sometimes I'm up to ten and eleven o'clock at night working with the kids. This is enough for me and I'm satisfied."

Roslyn recognizes that all of her efforts as a stay-at-home mom for the past thirteen years have not resulted in the desired outcome that she was hoping for regarding her oldest son. But being a domestic warrior doesn't imply perfection. She's secure in knowing that she was always there and available when she was needed. Her son's present difficulties and failures are of his own making, and she will not assume responsibility for actions of which she has no control. She's philosophical about the reasons.

"I've loved my son as much as I could. We gave him everything that he needed. In the past year, we have devoted so much time trying to help him figure out what's wrong in his life. I've done my part. His father and I can't do any more without sacrificing the other children. The most difficult thing for me to do was to put my son out of the house. But it was necessary. I don't feel stressed about it anymore. I've prayed about it. And I've left that burden with the Lord."

For Roslyn, midlife continues to be a period of hard work bound by joyous returns and glorious anticipation of what the future will bring. She devotes a high level of energy to the needs of her husband and two remaining children. When she discusses the multifaceted roles that she performs in life, she describes herself as "a counselor, healer, teacher, and spiritual adviser to my family and friends." She also serves as financial guardian to her maternal grandmother and has a renewed sense of commitment to her father and stepmother. Roslyn is actively involved in the lives of her siblings, nieces, nephews, cousins, extended family members, and "fictive kin." She expresses a strong faith in God, her husband, and the strength of her marriage. And she has no regrets.

SHELLI'S PATHWAY

Shelli was in the midst of enjoying everything that her high corporate status had to offer. After her eight-month maternity leave, she returned to the job in full force. Over the next several years, she arranged daily child care, focused "a reasonable amount" of attention on the needs of her husband, and managed to keep abreast of extended family issues. At work, she continued her supervisory responsibilities and gained additional promotions and territory. While Shelli often felt as if she were juggling too many balls at the same time, she managed to achieve a delicate balancing act between conflicting needs in the personal and professional realms. An accidental occurrence during a meeting at corporate headquarters changed her life forever.

"I remembered that we gathered for a major restructuring meeting," she recalls. "A new managing company had bought out the utility company, and they called in all the senior managers to talk about new job responsibilities.

"By accident or act of God, I saw all the salaries for all senior personnel posted next to their positions on a chalkboard. Everybody was making more money than me! Managers with fewer employees under them and smaller territories were making thousands of dollars more than me. One young white male was getting paid almost twice my salary. Here I was sitting there always playing the role of the good little darkie. Always on time. Always committed. Always willing to give 110 percent. I was furious. I went to the new vice president and demanded immediate compensation. He tried to explain that he was in a difficult situation and could not make an adjustment for another six months. 'Let's see what you can do,' he said. It was an almost show-me attitude that I found insulting. I had worked for the company for sixteen years, only to discover that I was a victim of racial and sex discrimination."

Younger sisters often enter the workforce oblivious to race and gender discrimination. They are familiar with the history of racial and sexual bias, but often adopt a show-me attitude before they are convinced of its reality. However, once publicly humiliated, they develop an appreciation for the nature of the beast and can acknowledge that the struggle continues.

Shelli turned to her husband for support. He offered a compassionate listening ear. However, he reminded her that in corporate America "you get as much as you're worth." That attitude only fueled her anger. Intuitively, Shelli knew that she was worth as much, if not more, than her white male counterparts. She mustered up all of her courage and set about planning a strategy to make her move.

"I sent out my resume!" she asserted as if she were making a declaration of war on the enemy. "Before I knew it, I was offered a job with a $30,000 increase. I knew my worth. I felt that I had been vindicated. I started all over again with the high-powered, super black woman thing. I was just as successful at my new job. Just after I finished my first year there, I began to feel that I no longer wanted to be part of this rat race."

Much to everyone's surprise, Shelli quit her position and decided to return home. She wanted to devote all of her time to her daughter, her husband, and the needs of her aging mother, who showed signs of suffering from Alzheimer's. Shelli had decided to become a domestic warrior. And she had a lot of explaining to do.

"My husband was 100 percent supportive of my decision. He knew that our lifestyle would change. We talked about the loss of income and what it would mean to the family. I was concerned about my daughter's emotional and social needs. It was all the take-out menus stuffed in the kitchen drawer and the mounting pile of cheap, disposable kiddie toys that come in the Happy Meal boxes that finally put me over the top. What kind of childhood could she be having if we ordered take-out dinners five nights out of the week?

"I was flying down the highway to get home, to pick her up, to take her to some activity. She didn't have time to play because I was so busy trying to make her schedule fit into mine. I just didn't want to live that kind of life anymore.

"My family thought I was crazy. I had to explain to my young nieces and nephews why, after college and a successful career, I would decide to return home to be a housewife. Education is so important to black people. If you get it, you're supposed to use it. I was the first in the family to get a college degree. I had already proved my success as a professional woman. It's not like I couldn't go out there and make a living if I wanted to. But this is what I wanted to do."

Shelli was concerned about her daughter's upbringing, but she could also envision herself playing a larger role in the community. This gave her new role greater meaning.

"It wasn't just a matter of staying home to focus on my own child," she states. "The black children in this community need an advocate. More than 30 percent of all the black chil-

dren in the school district are classified as special-needs students. I want to do something about that. I spend time at the
school tutoring and monitoring what's going on. I think that's
an important role to play. Black kids without a good education
are never going to make it. I was thirty-nine when I stopped
working. I've never looked back."

Shelli is certainly right about one thing: the overwhelming belief in the African American community that higher education is the pathway to success. In the past, employment
opportunities were often denied to black folks. Apprentice-
ships in many of the skilled trades were heavily dependent
upon sponsorship through the "old boys' network," and none
of the old boys lived in our neighborhoods. Education is something that can never be taken away from you. And it remains a
strongly held belief that higher education can grant access to
previously restricted job opportunities in the upper echelons
of society.

In retrospect, Shelli acknowledges that her life was less
complicated before the birth of her child. She was happy as a wife
and professional woman. The family was comfortable financially
and was nurtured by the support and admiration they received
from family members and friends. It was a typical black urban
professional lifestyle. Shelli states: "We were able to give a lot of
financial support to the organizations that we believed in, but we
were not able to give a lot of time." Nevertheless, Shelli and her
husband were high-achieving role models, and the younger generation was encouraged to emulate their success.

The decision to have a child was carefully considered.
Both Shelli and her husband wanted to be parents. They were

socially, emotionally, and financially ready. Yet maintaining her niche as a blissful wonder was a challenging and stressful endeavor. Her career as a professional woman may have continued indefinitely if she had not been confronted with the reality of race and sex discrimination.

In midlife however, Shelli also possessed a sensibility about her own wants, needs, and desires as a woman. And she no longer had a need to prove anything to anybody. Shelli proclaimed herself to be a self-assured woman capable of validating her own worth. She quit her job, cut up her credit cards, and rearranged her life the way that she wanted it to be. Shelli developed the fortitude that was needed to adapt to a new lifestyle and, in the process, discovered that the blessings of midlife continue to unfold.

CHRYSTAL'S PATHWAY

When Chrystal turned thirty-five, she was a single-parent professional. She had not planned on being a divorcée with the responsibility of raising her only child alone, but she accepted the newfound sense of peace and tranquillity that her single-parenthood lifestyle offered.

Free from the pressures of an insecure spouse, Chrystal obtained her master's degree two years after her divorce was final. She had a good job as an educational administrator and felt that additional graduate-level training would assist her in pursuing her goal of becoming a full-time educational researcher.

Four years had passed since she was involved in a serious relationship, and she was not searching for a dream partner. She expected to remain single—a status that was not unfamiliar to middle-aged professional black women. In fact, it appeared to be the norm. At frequent outings in restaurants, theaters, professional meetings, and social gatherings, Chrystal took note of the number of seemingly polished, attractive, professional black women hanging solo.

Chrystal met Alfred in an unlikely setting, in a downtown club, and she never thought that the encounter would go beyond that first dance to her favorite oldies song.

"My first blush reaction was that he was not my type: a big redbone type of guy. I didn't know if he was older or younger, and I thought he probably didn't know how old I was." However, from the moment he first laid eyes on her, Alfred pursued Chrystal with a vengeance. He attached himself in every way possible, making certain that he became a permanent fixture in her life. Before long, he was aggressively playing the role of "lover, protector, and man of the hour."

Chrystal and Alfred's courtship lasted five years. He was a frequent visitor to her home. As personal items began to pile up in her house, Chrystal recognized that Alfred was spending more time at her place than his own. While he continued to maintain a separate dwelling, they finally accepted the reality of their shacking-up arrangement and combined their resources in support of one dwelling.

Alfred and Chrystal had much in common. Both had learned about life's harsh experiences through previous relationships. Both had experienced marriage and divorce at a relatively young age and were skittish about making the same mistake twice. Moreover, in addition to Chrystal's daughter, Alfred was very much devoted to his own school-age children and fully committed to playing an active and supportive role in their lives.

Chrystal was ambitious. She wanted to continue her education and pursue loftier career goals. She played an active role in professional associations and in the community. Her ability to engage in multiple roles and perform multiple tasks provided a richness and fullness to her life. It added depth, meaning, and a sense of satisfaction that was previously absent. She was unwilling to make sacrifices. And Alfred never asked her to do so. He never questioned her involvement in activities and, in fact, encouraged her.

After five years of testing the waters, Chrystal and Alfred were married. The elaborate African-inspired ceremony was a public statement of their decision to remain committed to one another for the rest of their lives. Shortly thereafter, Chrystal returned to school and completed her doctorate degree. After twenty-three years of security in an administrative staff position, she quit her job and accepted a faculty appointment with the State University of New York.

Before embracing her role as a blissful wonder, Chrystal had experienced the love and loss of one marriage. She attributes much of its demise to youthful immaturity and the inability to separate her own desires from those that were socially imposed. Enduring a lengthy period as a single-parent professional would have sufficed if Alfred had not come along.

But as Chrystal matured, she had a better sense of self and found great comfort in the decisions that she made about the direction of her life. And, in her view, it was one of the greatest benefits of midlife: You know what you want to do with your life and you go out and do it.

As Chrystal eased into a new role and new career, she voluntarily withdrew from some social and professional activities that demanded too much of her attention. Deadbeat acquaintances were also eliminated as part of the excess baggage that no longer served a purpose in her life. She set limits on new social and personal endeavors and set about balancing the three most important priorities in her life: her husband, her children, and her career. Now comfortably in the throes of midlife, Chrystal enjoys the reward of a blissful wonder. She is fully devoted to her family and to a career that affords her the promise of continued professional development.

AYANNA'S PATHWAY

Ayanna's children are "halfway in and halfway out" of the nest. Her divorce at the age of twenty-eight forced her to make some adjustments in her life. "I'll never say that I wanted to be a single parent," she insists, "but I would argue that it's probably my greatest achievement to say that I was able to raise my two children alone after their father left." Ayanna has been a single parent for slightly more than a decade. She remains positive and philosophical about her experience.

"There were times when I thought that I was suffering all by myself. Once I got over having my pity party, I was determined to do my best. *I Will Survive* is the tape I played over and over again. At first, things started to fall apart. My finances were in a mess before I was able to pull myself together. I didn't want to ask anybody for help because I knew that they were not in the position to offer it. I was never destitute. I'm a professional woman quite capable of taking care of myself. But I could have used more help with the children."

There were deliberate choices that Ayanna made about her life and her future. She recognizes past errors, but prefers to focus on the positive outcomes. And, with clarity of vision, she's determined to stay the course. Even as she considers searching for a male companion, she remains lucid about her own standards. She refuses to settle for "the first available man that comes along."

"I've made some dumb decisions," she confesses. "I've gotten involved in relationships that I regret. I'm not at all sure how women with children date. I've met interesting men; some showed a lot of promise. But at my age, everybody has baggage. Some men have baggage and poverty working against them. They need all of their money to take care of the wife and kids that they left behind in their previous relationship. One guy had already been married twice and had five kids. As soon as you start to get close, they want to move into your house and let you help take care of them. I'm not going to raise another child.

"Trying to find 'Mr. Right' was always very awkward for me. I felt like I didn't want to sacrifice my kids for my sexual needs. When my daughter was about thirteen, she asked me if I wanted to get married again. She didn't give me a chance to answer. She told me that she didn't want to be a stepchild. It really had an impact on me. I started to feel like this was not the best time in my life to start dating someone new. And I don't think that all the book knowledge about the psychologically damaging effects of divorce on children helped me to move forward in that direction."

"I'm not waiting on Prince Charming. I've experienced a lot of toads already, and I knew they were toads when I let them in. I prefer to sit back and wait until the kids are out of the way. I discovered the pleasures of being a single mom and a free and independent black woman. The last few years with my children have been wonderful. If I die tomorrow, there would be no need to mourn for me. Just look at my children and remember that I did that.

"I'm perfectly happy with the ways things are. The last ten years have been great and the next ten will be even better. Forty is going to be a lot better than I expected."

Ayanna's happiness and sense of satisfaction in the beginning phase of midlife stem from the close relationship that she has with her two children. She continues to practice as a psychotherapist and plans to return to school in the near future. She lives a comfortable life because she prepared herself, educationally and emotionally, "to stand on my own two feet." Ayanna never regretted her decision to focus the bulk of her energies on the needs of her children. This was her all-consuming task for most of her thirties. "Once this part is over," she states rather confidently, "I can do my own thing—

that's anything I want to do. I can become a brand-new person." And it will be done with the satisfaction of knowing that she has performed admirably as a single working parent.

RICKI'S PATHWAY

Like Ayanna, Ricki decided that after two failed attempts at marriage, she was not about to sacrifice the needs of her child, or herself for that matter, to attempt a third marriage. Affairs of the heart would be placed on hold while she focused her attention on child rearing and her career. She was involved in loving relationships with significant others. In fact, one long-term relationship contributed significantly to her emotional well-being, as well as that of her daughter's. And it was her daughter's welfare that remained her top priority.

Ricki was experiencing some of the best times of her life. Yet she started to yearn for something else. Ricki wanted to pursue her lifelong dream and passion to live abroad and establish herself as an international citizen. She had proven her success as a journalist. She was a seasoned professional with twenty-five years of experience when she decided to throw in the towel on her journalistic career. Ricki pulled up stakes in the spring of 1998 and, with her ten-year-old daughter, moved to Paris, France.

"I've always dreamed of going to Paris and living there," she reports enthusiastically. "I knew I could enjoy living the life of an expatriate." She established living quarters in the heart of the city and set about creating a new venture on her own. As a skilled journalist, she had many avenues to pursue. But Ricki decided to strike out in a new direction. She released her entrepreneurial spirit and gave birth to Black Paris Tours.

Black Paris Tours is a successful one-woman tourist business that arranges sight-seeing tours, primarily for American tourists. These visitors travel to landmark locations made famous by the residencies of African American artists. The haunts of Josephine Baker, James Baldwin, and Henry O'Tanner are just a few of the celebrity locations on the tour.

The last three years in Paris have been wonderful for both Ricki and her daughter. Sacrifices have been made, but the rewards have been many.

"You make choices" states Ricki. "My daughter has blossomed here. She attends the regular public school, excels in her studies, and speaks French fluently. We have our own African American support circle. I would say that there's a strong community here. I've never been happier. You have to be secure enough to follow your dreams. Go for it. Take the chance." For Ricki, living in Paris was a dream nurtured in youth; midlife provided the opportunity to act on one of her greatest passions.

DARLA'S PATHWAY

There are times when a relationship with a significant other becomes the most important force in your life. The ability to achieve an overly indulgent, emotionally symbiotic relationship is highly desired by some. Others may find the appearance of a sugar-soaked, honey-dipped love-fest between two middle-aged adults nauseating. But there are many different roads to happiness.

Passionate soul mates are fully invested in the relationship and express great joy in existing in a world that grants them the opportunity to be "emotionally naked" in the presence of a loved one. As black women, they categorize their love as a "rare exception" and treat the relationship as sacred.

Darla's life as an independent free floater left little to be desired. She was as successful and as happy as any sister wanted to be. In many ways, Darla, as a young woman, paved the road to her life as a serendipitously satisfied human being. At the age of eighteen, Darla asserted her right not to be a Negro. She would forge her own identity and shape her life in ways she deemed satisfying. Never afraid to take a leap forward, Darla tested the waters of intimacy when and how she wanted. She changed career paths when she felt professionally and intellectually unchallenged, and changed the rules of the game when she felt that they were not in the interest of black women or black people. She was a willing learner and a perpetual student, never too arrogant to assume that "trying to teach an old dog new tricks" was not worth every bit of time invested.

When Darla turned forty, she thought about her future and the kinds of things that she had accomplished. Single and childless by choice, Darla could spend her time, money, and resources any way she pleased. And she did. She took frequent vacations back and forth to the West Coast and to the Caribbean. She drove a late-model car and lived in a fashionable townhouse in the downtown section of the city. She was a collector of African art and fine crystal. She was always impeccably dressed. Within her own circles she was the highest-paid and highest-ranking black female in local government. She donated to black charities and did volunteer work for the church and the community. She attended political action meetings and voiced her concern about the plight of the people. It was at one of those late-night meetings that she first met Conrad.

Conrad was a seasoned city administrator and political activist. He cared as much about the plight of the people as Darla. He frequently spoke out of turn to address the issue on the floor. Darla was not impressed. Several months later, she encountered the rabble-rouser at another political gathering. This time he was in charge of the meeting. Darla could see that he was somewhat bright, but she had not yet determined if he was quite on her level.

"I remember thinking to myself that I could do a much better job of handling the meeting than Conrad," she reminisces. "Men tend not to be as organized as women. They need to talk loud and spend time pontificating before they can get the job done."

Darla and Conrad moved around each other, sparring intellectually and testing each other's knowledge and positions on the major issues of the day. It was not a romantic attraction. If Conrad was interested in getting something started, Darla was not a good choice. Conrad was struggling with middle-age baggage. He had been married for more than twenty years and separated for two. He was contemplating divorce. He had a big mortgage, credit-card debt, and other bills to pay. Tuition bills loomed on the horizon and there were complex financial arrangements that needed to be implemented to ensure that all of his affairs were in order.

Darla had none of that; she was free and unencumbered. While Darla had experienced many relationship downers, she was always able to pick herself up, brush herself off, and keep moving forward. When she finally agreed to a first date, it was just something to do to pass the time.

Darla was attracted to Conrad for all the right reasons. He had a sharp mind that offered stimulating thoughts and conversation. He was only a few years older and clearly appreciative of the finely developed attributes of mature women. As Darla matured, she was well aware of the need that middle-aged men had to take up with younger women. But Conrad was a brother who was willing to play in his own backyard.

Darla and Conrad wanted the same kinds of things. As radical political activists, they were willing to spend their free time engaged in grassroots organizational efforts. It was a meeting of the mind and spirit. The more time they spent together, the more attached they became to one another. Friendship turned into love, and love grew into passion. After seven years together, nothing is more important in Darla's life than Conrad.

"This is absolutely as good as it gets," she gushes. "Our lives are so intertwined that it's hard to separate one from the other. Yes, we both do still have jobs. And I would say that I'm effective as ever. But Conrad is at the center of my life. I am a reflection of him and he is a reflection of me." After more than twenty-five years of fiercely asserting her independence, Darla fervently embraced the role of passionate soul mate. It is a role that she could not, and would not, embrace in her earlier years.

Whenever Darla mentions Conrad's name, she is effervescent and full of platitudes. She exudes joy and happiness like a nineteen-year-old June bride. But she is not. She is a middle-aged woman who has shaped her own destiny. And Darla is not alone. Other sisters have embraced the role of passionate soul mate in the middle stage of life. Not all have been as successful at keeping legal unions at bay while searching, albeit passively, for the perfect partner. Darla's story is representative of those who believe that, for mature black women, making the right love connection on your own terms is still within the realm of possibility.

SISTER WISDOM

Sisters with satisfying lives are frequently the ones who continue to recognize that life is an ongoing process. The sense of joy and merriment that they feel about their current stage of development rests on their understanding of the following valuable life lessons:

- *Love the ones you're with.* There's power in positive human relationships. Use it. Give and receive love. Affection is infectious, and it makes you feel good all over.
- *Never "settle" for anything.* Searching for a soul mate is a lengthy process. Experiencing life with-

out a partner can be lonely; getting hooked up with the wrong person is even worse.

- *Clarify your love of self before sharing it with others.* If you are unable to love yourself, others will have difficulty doing the same.
- *Continue to dream your dreams as you work your way toward gaining greater fulfillment in life.* Enjoy the life you're living, but continue to anticipate that greater rewards are just over the horizon. Plan ways to get there.
- *Get rid of the clutter.* The ability to find peace and happiness is within your reach. If you cannot find the pathway to this peaceful plateau, check out your surroundings. Chances are, too much clutter surrounds you.

8

Spiritual Fulfillment: "The Lord Works in Mysterious Ways"

All cultures have explanations of the beginning of the universe, the existence of God or Creator, and the promise of life after death. Traditional African religions speak of the spirit of the ancestors and the powerful existence of the living dead. Christians offer eternal life through the acceptance of Jesus Christ. And Muslims promise Heaven and eternity following a lifetime of dedicated service and commitment to Allah.

Female worshipers dominate the black church. Black women's faith, spirituality, and relationship with organized religion have been viewed as sources of strength and weakness. And they remain powerful currents in the black female experience.

For these mature sisters, the Jesus revival is alive and well. An all-consuming belief in their faith in God helps them to persevere in times of trouble. While sisters who are backsliders disparagingly describe this phenomenon as "pimping off the Lord," black women have never been shy about their belief in the power of the spirit. "Look to the Lord and He will provide!" And, for those whose cups are still empty, "the Lord's blessings are on the way!" While the search to find one's spiritual center may begin as early as adolescence or young adulthood, it tends to intensify with the passing of the years. This is certainly the case for sisters. Given the wretchedness of the human condition, finding one's faith, religion, or spirituality may be the essential tools needed for emotional survival. And sisters expressed varying degrees of commitment to their religious and spiritual beliefs.

THE POWER OF THE SPIRIT

Nashea lives a comfortable and satisfying material life. But that is simply not enough. She talks about her faith as an integral part of her being.

"I wouldn't be where I am today if I didn't have a strong spiritual foundation," she proclaims. "My life is centered around my beliefs. You carry yourself in a different way and project a different attitude when you know God."

Roslyn, too, is a believer. She uses prayer when overwhelmed by life's circumstances and considers herself a good Christian woman who attends church service as frequently as possible.

"I am a member of the AME church around the corner," she says. "I don't go as much as I would like to. There are just too many other things that I have to do. I try to leave Sunday as a day to do enjoyable things with my family and my kids."

Jocelyn, who has finally recovered from the emotional, social, and financial devastation following her divorce after eighteen years in an unhappy marriage, puts it this way: "I owe it all to my Lord and Savior, Jesus Christ, who I know has put me where I am today. I could not have survived without the comfort of the Lord. It is my faith in Jesus Christ that has allowed me to raise my daughters. . . . It's the love of my daughters that brings me the greatest joy. I'm truly blessed."

Darla is a practicing Baptist. She heads off to church every Sunday. Her absence from church service is explained by "being out of town on a business trip." Darla participates in church-sponsored activities and shares her expertise with the congregation and surrounding community members. According to Darla, "There is no doubt that there's a God. I've been blessed many times over and I never question His existence."

Shelli is not so sure. "I'm my own kind of believer," she offers cautiously. "You don't want to be in the position to question God. Some of my ambivalence I've picked up from my father. When something good happens, I always say 'thank God.' My father says, 'God didn't do that. You did that. Why thank God for something that you've done?'

"I belong to a church and attend on a regular basis. I was raised in the church and I want my child raised in the church. My husband and his people are quite religious. But just the other day I said to the minister, 'You have to forgive me for expressing my beliefs in ways that seem different from the Bible.' Some of the things the church cares deeply about—I don't think that God cares about them at all. All of this fuss about cutting your hair or dancing on certain days—I don't really think that God gives three hoots about that. I believe some of the stuff in the Bible. But some of it is a bit too far-fetched for me to accept. Like Jesus took five loaves and fed five thousand people. Really! If other people want to believe that, it's fine with me. I just have to come up with my own reasoning. Yes, there is a God. And if you do good deeds, that's enough."

Chrystal was raised a Catholic. She still recalls catechism lessons and can recite the "Hail Mary" at the drop of a dime. She abandoned her beliefs in Catholicism years ago and is quite uncertain about what she believes. She does not attend church on a regular basis. When she thinks about her spiritual life, she acknowledges that something is missing.

"I believe in God. I believe that I have a personal relation-ship with God. People look at me and say, 'You don't go to church?' I know I should be doing something about it—I just don't know what that is. The last time I attended church, I was reminded of the rigidly structured gender roles. There's too much deference to males and male authority. I can't get into that."

When Ayanna's husband walked out of her life, he took her faith with him.

"I attended church as a young girl," she recalls. "I went to Sunday school and vacation Bible school. I've always known that there is a God. I was raised a Baptist and taught all the things I'm supposed to know about Jesus Christ. It was a course in college that started me to think about the Lord in different ways.

"When I was a sophomore, I took a course in comparative religions. For the first time in my life, I was exposed to differ-ent religious philosophies. I didn't realize that other people had such different ways of explaining the world. When I thought of religious differences, it meant different Protestant denominations. How come the Baptists did this and the Methodists did that? How come the Lutherans and Episcopalians weren't in my neighborhood? And the Catholics were a separate entity all to their own. They were always kneeling in front of a cross or Mary or something. When I heard about the Jews and the Muslims and the Buddhists, I became confused. And where did black people fit in all of this?

"The divorce only made me angry about the behavior of 'good Christian men.' I haven't been back to church yet."

Olivia had a strong Christian upbringing in Boston. She recalls going to church every Sunday with her family or her cousins who lived in nearby Cambridge.

"There were a lot of different churches for black people. Because I was able to go to different churches every Sunday, I could see how people worshiped. There were three or four major black churches in Cambridge. I remember Union Baptist, Twelfth Baptist, and Saint Paul's. Well, it's the class distinctions that I remember more than anything else. It was like a caste system. Union Baptist was for the people down the West End. They thought they were a little better than the ghetto folks that went to Saint Paul's Church. And all the black ethnic groups were also in the mix. There were many West Indian families, some of whom had been there for a hundred years. I remember people talking about it as if one group was better than the other. But church life was important."

She stops long enough to reflect on where she is now and the best way to describe her spiritual life.

"Actually, I haven't been to church in years," she acknowledges. "There are only a handful of black people who live in this entire community. I'm not going to worship with white folks. I need a little more spiritual substance than that."

Forty-four-year-old Marlene is a successful entrepreneur and business owner. Her firm specializes in making small businesses technologically competitive. She voices her strongly held views on religion and the role that black women play in supporting the church.

"I live here in Atlanta," she states. "I see these sisters jumping on and off of buses to get to church or to hear some minister give them the word. They don't seem to be able to pull themselves together to get to work on time, or to do the kinds of things that would lead to improvements in their lives, but they will pull their pennies together and give it to some minister.

"We have this preacher down here. . . . He draws thousands of people to his ministry every week. Lots of poor people who don't have anything. But he wears Armani suits, drives a Cadillac, and owns a jet. And it's all being supported mainly by black women. I can't be bothered with that kind of foolishness.

"I believe in God. I pray and give money to the needy. But you won't find me in any of these churches."

A TEST OF FAITH

Other sisters tell stories of how their faith has been put to the test. Hazel represents one of many. She is forty-two years old and enjoys a good life. A public health nurse with a master's degree, she spends much of her time administering to poor white, black, and Hispanic families in need of health and educational supports. She has experienced many ups and downs in her life. She was a wild woman in her twenties. She was married, gave birth to a daughter, and then divorced. She experimented with life and partied away too much of her time. She began to settle down in her mid-thirties, furthering her education and finding the right professional position. Before long, she found a new partner, remarried, and found the Lord.

"I knew Jesus," Hazel proclaims, still in a highly agitated, emotional state. "I was in the church, saved. I can quote you the Bible and tell you the meaning of the scriptures. There was no one more into the Lord than me."

Hazel's faith was put to the ultimate test when her only daughter was rushed to the hospital complaining of pain in the abdomen. She was treated and sent home. Four hours later, she was dead.

"I called on Jesus. I asked that he save my baby, my one and only child. He did nothing. Why me? Lord, why me? Jesus has worked miracles. Why not work a miracle for me?"

Hazel's loss of faith may be temporary, but the tragic loss of her daughter is all too real. Her tragedy is compounded by painful thoughts of the wrongful death of a young black woman. Hazel has always known that being black can be hazardous to your health. She has often lectured to her clientele about how racial considerations follow you from birth to the grave. When Hazel considers the untimely death of her daughter, she wonders: *Why was her child sent home? Why wasn't her pain taken more seriously? Would the treatment have been the same for a young white female?* Hazel continues to be overwhelmed by grief. Floods of support continue to be offered by family, friends, and members of her congregation. She's inconsolable.

"People tell me to come to church," she cries out. "To pray. To take my pain to the Lord. What good is it going to do me now?"

FAITHFUL FOLLOWERS

While many of the sisters who participated in this investigation talked about their faith, most would not be described as faithful followers. As I said earlier, faithful followers are sisters who believe that they derive their strength, direction, salvation, and solutions to all problems from God. The power of religion is overwhelming to sisters on this pathway. Faithful followers are deeply spiritual and believe that God is in control of their lives. As black women, they are embracing a legacy of faith that has anchored the black community for centuries. Nothing happens without the blessing of God. And He provides all that is needed to enjoy a rich and satisfying life.

The eighty thousand sisters in attendance during the summer of 2000 at Bishop T. D. Jakes's conference, *Woman, Thou Art Loosed*, in Atlanta, Georgia, were undoubtedly faithful followers. They came to hear the word, to express their faith in God, and to share in the fellowship with other women accepting of the teachings of Jesus Christ, our Lord and Savior. Bishop Jakes is a fiery Protestant minister with Pentecostal flair. His conference speaks specifically to the painful sufferings of women and draws participants of different faiths from around the world. He has captured the hearts and imagination of thousands of Christian believers, both men and women. His primary message: With God, all things are possible. Sisters in attendance talked about "purging" their pain and seeking help in "lifting this heavy burden from my shoulders." According to one sister, who had traveled by van from Memphis, Tennessee, with four other church members and their children: "The reverend knows how to get to the deep-down pain that we black women are experiencing. He touches it [the pain] in a way like nobody else can do. I know that's why I'm here." And it was the voice of the spiritual needy that resonated throughout the three-day conference. In times of trouble, sisters seek comfort and solace in their spiritual centers. Once uncovered, faith is a powerfully potent, life-affirming force.

TERRI'S PATHWAY

As Terri entered midlife, she was still on a wild ride. She was quite innocent when she left home at eighteen to study at Spelman College in Atlanta. Her seven years on the police force provided an eye-opening, life-altering experience. After returning home to Alabama, she was fortunate enough to find a young lover, remarry, and have three additional children. But she also had been a partying, drug-abusing sister for more than twenty years.

Some aspects of Terri's life were perfectly stable. She had been with husband number two since she returned home. She had four children under her care. She lived in a three-bedroom home that she owned, through inheritance, and managed to survive with the aid of a few government programs. Terri was a functional abuser. For more than two decades, she enjoyed different types of recreational drugs. It was a problem she struggled with since her early days in Atlanta, but she always managed to survive. Things were never really good or really bad. Nothing was able to turn her life around, except the power of God. For Terri, His name is Allah.

For the past five years, Terri has been on the path to righteousness. Free of drugs for the first time in her adult life, Terri is thankful that finally she has been able to see the light. And much has changed since the day she heard the words that led her to salvation.

"I heard the teaching of the Honorable Elijah Muhammad," she confesses, "and that's what turned me around. There was a new set of rules that I had to follow. It is what is termed *restrictive law*. There was a lot of stuff we had to give up. We can't smoke tobacco, we can't smoke reefer, we can't get high, and we can't drink. These are things that I did before with a passion. I did whatever it was and whatever was available. But I was turned around by the grace of God."

Having been raised a Baptist, Terri is flexible about her religious beliefs. She does not attend services on a regular basis, but remains anchored in her faith in God and has embraced the spiritual side of life. Terri's persistent drug use had a substantial impact on her family and children during critical stages of development. She admits that her teenage son is having major social adjustment problems. However, on this day Terri expresses a renewed sense of dedication and commitment to family life. Concern over the quality of education has helped Terri turn her attention to home schooling. Her youngest child, now seven, is the primary beneficiary of her efforts. As we concluded the interview, Terri discussed the family's preparation to attend the Million Family March in October 2000. They want to make a statement about the importance of black family preservation and unification.

For Terri, midlife is a period of growth and renewal. It is also a time of tremendous change. Her ability to embrace the role of a faithful follower has fundamentally altered every aspect of her being. Terri openly acknowledges that after years of dependency on mind-altering substances, she has finally kicked the habit. She is leading a good life. And she owes it all to God. She had a choice to make about her future: more drugs or more faith! She chose God.

There are daunting social and emotional pressures that Terri continues to face from day to day. Her social resources are limited and her material needs are plentiful. But Terri is certain that God will provide. He will lead the way. He has restored her faith in her ability to survive, drug-free, in a challenging world. She is living proof of the power of the Lord. In Him, all things are possible.

KALILAH'S PATHWAY

It had been more than ten years since Kalilah's divorce from her fifth husband. True to her word, she promised herself that she would not marry again. Kalilah had several loving, long-term involvements, but she resisted their proposals of marriage. Her two children were out on their own and she was proud of their achievements. She was now a grandmother and looked forward to spending time with the newest addition to the family.

Just after Kalilah turned forty, she decided to give up her secrets and share her pain with her brother, from whom she had grown distant since the incident in the garage when she was just seven years old.

"I can remember how my relationship with my brother changed after the incident in the garage. I stayed away from him. I was so afraid that he would find out that I couldn't be close to him. I was afraid that I might slip up and tell him what happened."

Kalilah's revelation brought her some relief, but it didn't make her happy. As she approached her mid-forties, she continued to question the meaning of life. She found her answer one day while watching TV. It was an afternoon talk show. The host was Oprah Winfrey.

"One day, I was watching *Oprah*. And they were talking about a twelve-step program. And they were saying that in order to be successful, you had to give over your life to God. You had to turn over your life to God for Him to run. I thought to myself, *You can't give over your life to anybody*. And then it hit me. *When did I get so far away from God?*" As Kalilah talks about the revelation she had that day, she explains how everything started to change. And for the first time in many years, she was overwhelmed with a sense of joy, peace, and satisfaction. She euphorically explains:

"God is my life. I don't take a step without first consulting with Him. I get up in the morning and I pray. Before I go to bed at night, I pray. I pray while I'm at work, and sometimes I pray two or three more times a day. I read the Bible at night. I truly, truly rely on God. I grew up as a Catholic. After I was on my own, I became a Muslim. I just wandered or maybe drifted away from Islam.

"I don't go to church. It's just me and my Bible and God. I have no qualms about anybody else's religious beliefs. It doesn't matter if you're a Buddhist, Muslim, or Christian. If you believe in God, you're a friend of mine."

It has taken Kalilah nearly fifty years to arrive at this place. For the first time in her life, she feels capable of accepting herself as a whole person and affirms the fundamental value of her worth as a human being. Her relationship with God has given her strength.

SISTER WISDOM

As we mature, faith assumes a more significant role in our lives. Indeed, for faithful followers, it is the love of God that makes a joyous life possible. They embrace the power of the Lord and are at peace with their decision. Faith manifests itself in many ways. But there is one lesson that we can all learn from the experiences of these sisters: Now is the time to get your spiritual house in order. Your spiritual beliefs help you to make sense of the world. Force yourself to be clear and specific on what you believe and why you believe it.

9

Free as We Want to Be

Well, you know that Whitney Houston song "I'm Every Woman"—I feel a little bit like that. At my fortieth birthday party, I couldn't believe how good I felt and how good I looked. I wasn't born with a silver spoon in my mouth, but I made some pretty good choices. I would say that I got my own silver platter. I took advantage of every opportunity available. I went to day school and night school. I changed my job when the opportunity was right. I wasn't afraid to take a leap. While most of the people that I grew up with didn't leap with me, I still feel like I accomplished a lot as a black woman. After too many failures, I finally found the man of my dreams. He's twenty years older, but I can live with that. Now

I can stop being selfish and think about giving back.
I've still got time to make some good things happen.
—Yolanda, age 41

The ability to make it, succeed, and live large in America is a familiar story for black women who have carved out their own special niche as independent free floaters in a world of unequal opportunity. Hard work and sacrifice tell part of the story; the contributions and encouragement from a host of supporters—from family and friends to elders and ancestors—tell the rest. These sisters have overcome many social and cultural obstacles to demonstrate their ability to achieve against all odds. Yet they speak proudly as beneficiaries of a bygone era, and are mindful of the opportunities granted to some members of this generation but denied to many others. And, in the words of one sister, "I'm just hitting my stride."

The spirit of triumph, the feeling that "it's my time," as expressed by many sisters who feel that they are enjoying satisfying lives, epitomizes the lifestyle of the independent free floaters. As black women, they recognize that they are among the largest cohort of a single, successful, unencumbered adult population in the United States, with plenty of money. And they spend it any way they please.

OLIVIA'S PATHWAY

When Olivia thinks about her impending thirty-ninth birthday, she confesses, "I can deal with this. I can see that I'm in a wonderful position. I'm financially independent, live in a comfortable home, and have a solid career. Nothing's secure forever, but the material things that were so important to me before no longer seem to matter.

"I remember just a few years ago when I decided to leave my position and take another job in an area where there were very few black folks. It no longer seemed to matter that I would not live in the heart of the black community. I prefer to live around my own people, but sometimes you make a decision to go where there's additional opportunity.

"I was thinking that if I were married with children, I would not have been able to make the move. And then I thought about how much time sisters spend obsessing about the lack of available partners for black women. None of that matters anymore. I'm happy with who I am and the direction that I'm going in. This place where I'm living lacks community, but I know how to take care of that. I have sister friends all over the country. Some from my childhood years, others from college, some in my sorority, and a few I've met through the workplace. I have a strong network of sisters. I depend on these sisters to nurture me, to give me the social and spiritual input that I need to make it through this crazy world. I often say that if I were a lesbian, I would be like a hog in pig heaven. The sisters are always there for me."

Olivia is a research biologist. She spends her time working, traveling, and enjoying her sister friends. Her future is bright, unclouded by dreams of what she hopes to be, but with a great acceptance of who she has become. She anticipates that the added maturity of midlife will bring a bountiful harvest in all realms of life. Olivia is no longer stressed about the need to procreate. She made a decision early in life that she would not have children without the benefit of marriage. And she is satisfied that she made the right choice. However, she is considering adoption. She states: "I have an awful lot that I could give to a child in need."

TEA'S PATHWAY

Tea has been enjoying life as a single woman for more than fifteen years. After ten years of marriage to a perfectly good man, Tea and her husband agreed that it was time to move on. They parted amicably. He could pursue his dreams and she would follow her heart. New York was big enough for the two of them to carve out their own separate spaces.

Dreams of being a famous rhythm and blues singer like Frankie Lymon, who she idolized as a child, had long since faded. But Tea's love for the arts endured. In between working and trying to raise her son as a single parent, Tea managed to go back to school and get a graduate degree. With a master's degree from Columbia University, she could rightly claim that she was Ivy League. As she entered her mid-forties, Tea realized that she could be much more effective as a producer rather than an entertainer. As an independent free floater, Tea decided to write her own script.

"I don't want anybody to control my life. I could see what was happening to black people in the industry, and I wanted to try to make some changes for the better. Producing allows me the opportunity to showcase black people, to tell our stories, to focus on the things that are important to us.

"I know that I'm successful. I travel all over the world and get to use my gold card. It's not the one from American Express—it's the one my mother earned for me because of all the sacrifices that she made that allow me to be where I am today.

"Dating is still a big part of my life. I want to find some- one to spend the rest of my life with. But I do have standards. You can't come to my house and put your foot up on the table when you're not putting anything on the table. I will not be your caretaker. I no longer care if the men that I date are black or white. In fact, most of the men that I've been seeing in the last several years are white men. Black men seem to be more threatened by my success. I don't have the time to struggle with all of that. I want my romantic life to be loving and sup- portive, not bitter and competitive."

As a highly successful fifty-one-year-old black woman, Tea paints a rosy picture of the years to some. She foresees greater opportunities in the production industry and increased access to professional venues that were previously closed to black peo- ple. For Tea, it's as if she were at the beginning of a great adven- ture, and, in her view, she's not even middle-aged yet.

NASHEA'S PATHWAY

Nashea was in her mid-thirties when, without warning, she abandoned her marriage to the wealthy European, gathered the belongings of her twelve-year-old son, and returned back home to Delaware. Nearly fifteen years had passed before she realized she had traded her youth and dreams of being an entrepreneur for the maturity and stability that a marriage offered. Within six months, she relocated to the Washington, D.C., area and reestablished herself as a financial consultant. She had selected the pathway of a single-parent professional and was determined to be an unqualified success.

If others view Nashea's actions as the beginning of a midlife crisis, she does not share this vista. This was not her moment, although she does recognize that she embarked on a new phase in life.

"I was a young woman with my whole life ahead of me," she explains. "My husband had given me every material thing imaginable. I didn't cook, I didn't clean, and I even had help raising my only child. What I didn't have was an identity all of my own. It was just time for me to move on. I wasn't feeling old, mature, or anything like that. I did feel a little bit wild and adventurous. That's how I was able to make the move." Nashea exudes a healthy dose of self-confidence. She's certain that she's on the right track. With an authoritarian edge to her voice, she sums up her current stage in life.

"Being middle age is a state of mind. I feel better now than I did ten years ago. I look as good as I did way back when. My skin is toned and my body tight. Nobody believes me when I say that I have a twenty-four-year-old son. Younger men are attracted to me and don't seem to mind at all that I'm an older woman. I'm not thinking of having any children, but all my body parts are still in the right place. This is a glorious time of life."

Hard work and dedication did result in Nashea's business being an unqualified success. Her six-figure income was more than sufficient to provide for the needs of her family. Nashea is a happy woman. She is where she wants to be and nothing interrupts her euphoric state of being. She is in full charge of her world and defiantly declares: "I'm creating my life instead of having someone create it for me."

RENEE'S CHOICE: BE BOLD ABOUT IT!

"I have something I want to tell you."

And that was about all that she said. Popular TV personality and coanchor of the channel 10 evening news, Renee Chenault beamed before the cameras as she announced to the viewing public that she would be sharing news about her life in less than a week.

The city was abuzz. What was the big announcement? An engagement soon to be followed by a wedding date? Who was the lucky guy? Or was it professional in nature? Would Renee be leaving News Ten in search of a better job? We were instructed to tune in on Monday if we wanted to hear the secret that she was about to reveal to the world.

Renee was one of the most visibly successful sisters in the city of Philadelphia. Slim, petite, and ravenously beautiful, Renee had made her mark as a politically astute newscaster in the local market. A graduate of the University of Pennsylvania Law School, she had forsaken a career in the legal profession to make her mark on the television airways. And she was good at it.

From outward appearance, Renee's life as a single professional black woman left little to be desired. She was the quintessential free floater. She had made it in a big way, and thousands of women admired her for her success and achievement. She was fully enjoying the prime of her life. But something was stirring in her soul. There was more to life than bright lights, fancy clothes, and fine restaurants. Life was good, but it could be even better. As she assessed her current situation, she saw a few changes coming over the horizon.

"I'm going to have a baby," she declared on the six o'clock news. But that was only part of the story. Renee's artificially inseminated pregnancy was the real news. For the next week, the public would be privy to the ins and outs of the in vitro fertilization procedure. As she carried us through the process and gauged the reaction of family, friends, and the public, we would gain insight about her decision to choose this technological approach to motherhood.

Renee made a bold move—one she described as "the right choice for me." She had chosen a lifestyle that suited her needs and desires. Her life would be transformed by the addition of her unborn child, and her status would change from single woman to single mother. But she was clear about her choice and confident in her ability to follow a pathway that offered a rewarding and satisfying life.

SOUL SURVIVORS

In many ways, all the sisters who shared their stories of trials, tribulations, and triumphs on the road to finding satisfying lives can be viewed as soul survivors. There is a common theme in the message that they all transmit: Regardless of what has happened in the past, a positive and fulfilling life is waiting ahead. There were personal challenges and social hurdles that had to be overcome before many were able to embrace their own desires and take control of their lives. Yet they all have emerged victorious.

Ricki set out to change the world by altering the negative perceptions of black folks in the media. Darla, Nashea, and Tea challenged gender restrictions at home and in the workplace. Ayanna overcame poverty and personal strife before she grew comfortably into the role of a single-parent professional. Roslyn remained devoted to her family. She kept a watchful eye on the educational system and its overzealous attempts to classify black children as special education candidates. At the same time, she struggled to understand the problems of drug addiction that consumed the life of her eldest child.

Before she turned her life over to God, Terri struggled with the socially devastating consequences of drug addiction. Kalilah battled "secret demons" most of her life. She sought happiness through multiple marriages. And bowing to the social pressures of youth, Kalilah was the consummate joiner for every major movement that engulfed the community as she searched for a comfortable identity.

Chrystal's expectations about women, work, love, and marriage sent her life in an undesirable direction before she declared her independence, claimed her own space, and set the parameters for her own happiness. Shelli battled corporation discrimination and conspicuous consumption before changing her priorities and refocusing her energies on her family. Many sisters faced battles against racial and gender restrictions in the workforce, educational institutions, and other social arenas. For black women, pressing social issues often translated into personal problems as the personal and political arenas began to collide.

But soul survivors are a special breed. In a sense, it's the life-threatening challenges that often force us to stop and count our blessings. *Things are tough!* we think to ourselves. But in the very next moment, we come to the realization that they could be far worse.

Soul survivors view life as a constant struggle but believe that they have the ability to overcome life's obstacles. They continue to push forward. They persevere. And they look back on their lives and celebrate the fact that they've come this far.

TARA'S PATHWAY

Tara, whose life was shattered by the revelation that her husband had molested her oldest daughter, is a soul survivor. She had very little opportunity to lament over her tragic difficulties before she discovered that she was suffering from a virulent and aggressive form of breast cancer. Yet Tara was able to turn her brief moment of helplessness into hope. She tapped her deep reservoir of inner strength and surfaced with an incredible amount of optimism about her life and her future.

"I've had thirty-six radiation treatments, several operations, and many uncertain moments . . . but I still feel blessed. I can't believe how having breast cancer can be such a positive force in your life. It has given me a purpose, a mission in life. I can see things more clearly now than I ever did before."

It's been a busy and productive life. She has organized a support group for women trying to make the transition from welfare to the workforce. She has edited and published a collection of personal narratives by women who have survived tumultuous times. At the time of the interview, Tara had just received a pink slip from her employer. It was a standard two-week notice that terminates her employment. She appeared unfazed by the pending loss of her position and remained optimistic about her ability to create a new job for herself.

Tara is an independent, strong-willed woman with well-honed survival skills. She is resolute in her commitment to remain productive and vital, and keeps a vigilant eye on her emotional and physical health. Maintaining a positive outlook on life is a top priority.

God, too, plays a role in Tara's life. Tara is strong in faith, but selective about how she supports the faithful. "I need to know where and how my money will support the needy," she says. "I'm a very spiritual person. I believe in God and doing what's right. You can't always be sure what your church donations are used for, but when you're directly involved in a program, it's easier to identify the needs. I want to be there, ministering to those in need." And sisters in need have discovered that they have a friend and advocate in Tara.

JUDITH'S PATHWAY

Judith's inner spirit beams with the same forceful rays of sunlight that undoubtedly shone upon her as a child in her seashore community. Judith, who learned of her interracial heritage on the school playground, never doubted the importance of her family legacy. From the very beginning, she had been reared to be an intelligent, high-achieving African American woman. The revelation of her father's German heritage, and his death when she was only twelve years old, didn't alter her course. She has no stories to tell about the "tragic mulatto." She was grounded in her blackness and buoyed by a strong sense of self from the very beginning. Judith is inextricably linked to a close-knit family that remained supportive throughout her life. Their support, coupled with her own sense of determination, led to the fulfillment of her professional goals. Her stellar career in public service is quite an accomplishment.

Not only was Judith able to thrive after the death of her father, but she repeatedly demonstrated her ability to survive mounting social and personal obstacles that challenged her throughout her life. She has been able to do so because she accepts life's inevitable tragedies and disappointments as learning experiences. They have served as building blocks to strengthen her fortitude and enhance her capacity to survive in a potentially hostile environment. It was a lesson imparted early in childhood when Judith was able to see the differential treatment directed toward the haves and the have-nots, the rich and the poor, the men and the women, and the blacks and the whites.

Judith views her failure to complete medical school as a triumph. She recognized her discomfort with medicine early in her training and voluntarily withdrew to pursue other goals. She pursued higher education with a vengeance. She obtained a college degree and dabbled in a number of professional arenas before deciding on a career in public service.

Pregnancy out of wedlock was not part of her original plan, but it was accepted as a blessing, and Judith moved on. While she had hoped never to struggle with problems of substance abuse in her own family, that would not be the case. Yet she clung tenaciously to all that was good about her husband and her marriage while they worked things out. And even in the face of a life-threatening illness, her courage has never wavered. Judith is a soul survivor.

Judith's struggle with her husband's substance abuse problems exacted an emotional and financial toll. When her health started to fail, she attributed much of her decline to stress associated with family disruption due to her husband's drug use. Physical examination revealed something else: breast cancer. It would present her with one of her major life challenges.

"Personally, I'm going through many health challenges right now," she states philosophically. Her elegant presence permeates the atmosphere. The details of her medical challenges are unnerving, but she continues to project a facade of strength and courage. Her confidence leaves you breathless, as if her inner life force has sucked up every available source of oxygen in the room. It's what she needs to continue to move forward.

"My body is changing on me. It is doing different things. People tell me I'm doing too much. Everybody else wants to run my life to tell me what I can and can't do. I tell them that they don't understand that this keeps me going. I have problems with one of my eyes. I've been going through that for a couple weeks. I had a lumpectomy about three years ago, and I'm going through that again. They just detached another tumor, and it's malignant. They're saying no more lumpectomies—we'll have to do something else. So to me, I'm going through these major health challenges right now, but I don't want anything to stop me. I just keep going."

Judith intends to fight the reoccurrence of breast cancer with every bit of courage that she can muster. "I just bought a new house in the city," she added, "and I'm already starting on my Rites of Passage program for next year." Judith uses the program to work with young sisters and brothers in need of special guidance. She believes that her active involvement with black youth is the only way to save the next generation.

"In just twenty years, I can see the difference between what I had as a child and what these young people are struggling with. Most are from single-parent homes. They have a parent or two on drugs, and they're just a moment away from being homeless. They know people who have been shot and murdered. I want them all to make it, but I know that some will not."

They will if she has anything to do with it. Reaching out to youth helps to balance her life. She is committed to young people and will serve as their role model and advocate as long as it is possible.

SISTER WISDOM

Believing that you've positioned yourself to start anew, fulfill your dreams, or just kick back and enjoy the fruits of all of your hard work and labor is a powerful place to be. Getting to that place proves to be more than a matter of simply aging. Making the right decisions and understanding the consequences are essential to the process. There are some lessons in life that serve you well at any stage of development:

- *Live your life to the fullest.* Here today, gone today! Keep this in mind as a reminder of life's brevity.
- *Share your wisdom and life experiences with others.* Give something to the next generation. Whatever benefit others can gain from your strengths and weaknesses, let them have it. Remember, ancestors are those who live long lives and do good deeds. And years after they have passed on, members of the community can still recall their names.
- *Place yourself at the top of your priority list.* This is something that you should have done a long time ago, but it is never too late to get started. You deserve to treat yourself. Give unto you all that you would give unto others.

Most of these sisters are located exactly where they want to be. They are functioning at the top of their game and have earned the right to create a lifestyle reflective of their wants and desires. They have extracted the positive, essential elements from a bittersweet life and used them as building blocks for a brighter future.

Converting potentially devastating life experiences into stories of triumph is the common thread that runs through all the stories of these women, but especially those of soul survivors. They have a new purpose and mission in life. Like

Judith and Tara, sisters who are soul survivors recognize that each stage of life brings a host of challenges and obstacles that must be addressed forthright with courage and perseverance. There's a price to be paid for longevity. And midlife can serve as a sweet reminder that new beginnings are just beyond the horizon.

10

Sisters in the Prime of Life

Developing an appreciation for the enormous benefits of maturity and learning to value the gift of life were familiar themes that reverberated in the final moments of my interviews. These sisters are pleased with their many accomplishments and proud of their achievements. They have traversed a major milestone in their lives, reached a comfortable plateau, and are reaping the benefits of their new locations. They are hopeful about the future and envision more opportunities for personal and professional growth.

There's no one simple model that encapsulates the source of their pleasure. And their experiences are far from being monolithic. Ringing forth is the feeling of satisfaction derived from a strong sense of self and an acceptance of who they are as mature African American women. These are self-validating sisters who are centered in their own experience. They understand the essence of their being and would never forsake the identities that they have chosen for themselves to wear a mask that was designed by others. There is a high level of contentment that resonates throughout. You can hear it echo in their voices as they share their feelings about the prime of life.

According to Roslyn: "The prime is the point in your life when you can concentrate on yourself. You can do pretty much anything that you want. You are set financially, or as best as you can be, and you get to travel and enjoy life. When you're nineteen or twenty years old, you think that you are in your prime, but you're not. The prime comes when you're an older woman."

"The prime is at that point when everything is going well for you," says Shelli. "I feel that's where I am now in a sense. . . . You're not so much into climbing up the corporate ladder, but you are at a point where you are successful in your career. You're happy with that. You're successful in your family life, and you are happy with that. You are happy with your spiritual life. When all those things come together and you can look back and say to yourself, 'Hmmn . . . life is good,' that's when you know you're in your prime."

For Olivia: "I think the prime is when everything gets good and feels better. The trick is to know that you're in your prime before things start to sour."

While it required a deep moment of reflection, Ayanna, too, thinks she's about to enter her prime. "Yes . . . I guess that it's true, although I may not have responded that way before. I'm a well-preserved black woman. It's not just okay to be turning forty; it feels rather good. I can kick back and enjoy where I am right now. When you first realize that you're about to pass a major milestone, it gives you a little bit of the jitters. But once I grabbed hold of myself and took a good look at my life, I realized that I was more satisfied than I had ever been before. This is when you can enjoy your young adult children. You can pat yourself on the back for doing such a damn good job. It's when you're pleased with your job. It's when you stop thinking about all the things that you never really needed and appreciate all that you have. I think this is the prime."

Chrystal, a true reflection of her status as an educational researcher, describes the prime in textbook terms: "If you look at the curve of life, it goes up and comes back down. It represents life's continuum. The large top of the curve is when you're in your prime. If you believe that you're going to live until you're eighty—and I believe that I'm going to live until I'm eighty—you start to peak around forty or fifty. I see myself peaking at the top of the curve. I'm in my prime right now."

Judith got her lesson about the prime from an older colleague: "I was at a retirement dinner and the honoree said she was stepping down in the prime of her life. I asked her, 'What is the prime?' She said, 'It's when your worries and concerns are at a minimum. Things are just not going to get any greater or any worse than what they are right now. You are able to just step out on a daily basis and do what you gotta do.' I thought I was past my prime, but I guess I'm not there yet."

Daphne, the forty-eight-year-old grandmother with a boyfriend sixteen years her junior, knows that she is in her prime. She states: "The prime is when your kids are gone, when you've separated from your husband, and you can do anything that you want to. I'm definitely in my prime. I like doing me."

Marlene points out that the prime is "whenever you get to the point in your life when you no longer give a . . . about what other people are saying. There are two things that I will not tolerate from other people: comments about my hair and comments about my weight! When you reach your prime, you feel free to do anything that you want to."

For another fifty-five-year-old sister: "The prime is when one is at the peak of their physical, intellectual, and financial capabilities. I'm in my prime right now. I've got my education. It was the union card that got me out of poverty. I don't know if it's as good as it gets because it might get even better."

And Darla was more than willing to throw her understanding of the prime into the mix: "Well . . . let me put it this way. If this ain't the prime, then the prime must be awfully prime. I wake up in the morning and I think of two things: (1) Somebody pinch me. This can't be real. Or (2), something bad is about to happen. That's how good things are in my life right now. This supersedes everything that has come before it. I don't know what comes after, but this supersedes everything that has come before."

Nashea is looking forward to the prime. "The prime refers to people who are over fifty. It's when you're in a centered place in life. I haven't reached that place. I think when I'm about sixty, I might be able to describe that. I'm excited about where it's going to take me. But I want to know where it's going next.

"Everything that has happened so far has been good. And I'm also really centered spiritually. I'm really passionate about God. I'm in this place right now where I feel like God is leading me in everything I do.

"One of the reasons why I'm not looking for a serious relationship is because I have all these things together in this stage in my life. My father was a wonderful but very controlling man. I don't want to be over fifty and have to dedicate my life to someone else. I don't want to be a nursemaid. I don't want debt. I don't want drama. So that eliminates a lot of folks. I'm the kind of person that doesn't want anybody in my house.

"The most important things in my life right now are my spiritual beliefs and my ability to maintain myself financially. I'm in the position to give back. That's why I spend so much time with the high school kids. And I'm very passionate about my business and I'm working with young people around that.

"All of my life I have been different. I'm not one of those people who wishes that I could turn back the hands of time, because you can't. I don't want to be where I was twenty or thirty years ago. I want to be where I am right now. And I have no fear of growing older."

And forty-three-year-old Sharon puts it this way: "I figure the prime is a part of your life where you are doing what you want to do. You're enjoying yourself and you are fulfilling what you want to do. You've decided, *Okay, I want this and now I'm doing it.* When I was younger, I dibbled and dabbled at this and that, and didn't know what I wanted to do. When you hit the prime, you know exactly what you want and you do it."

SISTER WISDOM

These sisters are enjoying the prime of their lives. They have redefined their roles as black women in America and have charted a path for themselves that is richly rewarding and satisfying. They have left behind negative stereotypes and abandoned the mythical role of the superstrong black woman, but continue to possess the indomitable will and spirit of their foremothers. They exercise their right and freedom to choose their own roles. African American women are productive, contributing members to the African American community and American society. Yet most acknowledge that the struggle is not over. Social barriers must continue to fall. As a community, we must persevere in our fight against racist, sexist, and other discriminatory practices. And as sisters, we must make greater strides toward effectively mobilizing the sisterhood.

Consider the following guidelines:

- *Be as super as you want to be.* Maintain your strength and fortitude without being bowled over by the false belief that you can or should do it all.
- *Locate your spiritual center.* Faith is a powerful defense against emotional deterioration. Never leave home without it.
- *Have the courage to pursue your dream.* It's not possible to pursue someone else's dream. Seek your own balance and craft your own vision of the future.
- *Stand in a position of readiness.* Prepare yourself emotionally, educationally, and financially to stand

on your own. The ability to thrive and survive rests in your own hands.

- *Accept the social realities of being black and female in America.* Every day for the rest of your life you will awaken to the reality that you're a black woman. It's not going to go away. Keep your radar turned on. Fight against stereotypes. Fight to make it better for the next generation of young people.

- *Maintain a conscious awareness of heritage and legacy.* Educate yourself about the past and learn from those who survived in more perilous times. Spend an adequate amount of time with the elders. Consume their wisdom. It is invaluable, and they will give it to you for free.

- *Abandon dead-ends, dead weights, and deadbeats.* Unnecessary baggage will always stand in the way of your happiness, unless you leave the bags behind.

- *When life hands you a lemon, make an old-fashioned, down-home, throw-down, "put my foot in it," lemon meringue pie, with whipped cream and a cherry on top.* The ability to make something good out of a bad situation is what brought our foremothers to this place. And skip the guilt trip. You did the best that you could at that time.

- *Love thyself, want thyself, know thyself, and be thyself.* It's what makes life worth living.